WILDFLOWERS *of* ALASKA *and the* YUKON TERRITORY

Bearberry (*Arctostaphylos uva-ursi*)

STEVE CHADDE *and* LOUISE POTTER

Illustrations by EVA MELADY

AK **YT** refers to presence in Alaska or the Yukon Territory.

WILDFLOWERS OF ALASKA AND THE YUKON TERRITORY

Steve Chadde *and* Louise Potter
Illustrations by Eva Melady

ISBN 978-1951682934

A Pathfinder Field Guide
Published by ORCHARD INNOVATIONS
Mountain View, Arkansas
info@orchardinnovations.com

VER. 1.0 03/2025

CONTENTS

INTRODUCTION

WILDFLOWERS OF ALASKA AND THE YUKON TERRITORY is a field guide to more than 250 wildflowers commonly seen in Alaska and the Yukon. Rather than a simplistic arrangement by flower color, the plants are arranged alphabetically by the scientific name of the plant family (for example, Asteraceae, the Aster family). This places closely related plants together to make identification easier, and importantly, will help you become familiar with the characters of each plant family, so important in becoming skilled at identifying plants, no matter where you travel. General characteristics of each plant family are also provided in the **Family Synopses** (page 296).

From roadsides to coastal shores, to tundra, muskeg, forests and alpine regions, our hope is that this guide will be a valuable companion to anyone wanting to discover the surprising variety of plant life found in these northern latitudes.

USING THIS BOOK

Common (or English) names and scientific (or Latin) names are given for each species, followed by a non-technical description of the plant. Commonly used synonyms (formerly accepted scientific names) are provided. In some cases there is not universal agreement as to the correct scientific name, and an alternate name is useful to avoid confusion. Next, the plant's life-form (perennial herb, shrub, etc.) is given, followed by characteristics of its flowers, stems, and leaves. Note that plant heights are approximate only as there is great variation in a plant's stature depending on elevation, soils, microclimate, etc. Habitat information (where the wildflower is typically found) is provided, with additional details about a plant's use as food, or if it is considered dangerous and should never be eaten. As a general rule, no plant should be eaten before first verifying its safety with a knowledgeable person.

Each wildflower is illustrated with several color photographs depicting the plant's overall form, its leaves, and its flowers. In addition, a line drawing by botanical illustrator Eva Melady is provided to highlight important details of the plant. The small boxes with 'AK' or 'YT' indicate the plant's presence or absence in the state or territory. Remember, however, that the flora of Alaska and the Yukon Territory includes many more plants than are described here, and important groups such as the grasses (Poaceae) and sedges (Cyperaceae) are not treated (apart from several interesting and widespread species of cottongrass [*Eriophorum*]). Alaska boasts over 1,700 species of vascular plants, while nearly 1,300 are reported from the Yukon. To learn more about the region's flora, please see the **additional references** (both print and online) on page 314.

The use of technical botanical terms has been limited to those necessary to describe the plants basic flower, stem, and leaf characteristics. Technical terms used are defined in the **illustrated glossary** (p. 301), followed by an **index to plant families** (p. 318), and a **complete index** to both scientific and common names (p. 319).

ACKNOWLEDGMENTS

The original text of this book was based on co-author Louise Potter's *Roadside Flowers of Alaska,* first published in 1962. The entire text has been updated and revised to reflect current scientific names and family groupings, and more wildflowers have been added to make the book as comprehensive as possible.

Scientific names largely follow those of the Biota of North America Program (BONAP, *www.bonap.org*), and of the 'Plants of the World Online' database maintained by the Royal Botanic Gardens, Kew (*powo.science.kew.org*). Presence or absence in the region was verified using distribution maps generated using the Floristic Synthesis program by BONAP.

In addition to the line drawings from the original work, over 700 color photographs have neen incorporated into this volume. Nearly all photographs were obtained from the *www.inaturalist.org* website under the appropriate Creative Commons license allowing for commercial use; inaturalist is the leading community-driven site for sharing ecological data. Photographer names (as provided on inaturalist) are listed on each image. This book would not have been possible without their efforts to document our diverse flora.

WILDFLOWER DESCRIPTIONS

PARTRIDGEFOOT (LUETKEA PECTINATA)

ANDERS HASTINGS

SUSAN BLAYNEY

Blitum capitatum

STRAWBERRY-BLITE, STRAWBERRY-SPINACH

SYNONYM *Chenopodium capitatum*
Annual herb from a stout taproot. **Flowers** greenish, small globular 'crumbles' which turn red and berry-like as plant matures, terminal on a spike or from leaf axils. **Stems** erect (4–24 inches), smooth, branching from base. **Leaves** spear-shaped, pointed, broad, thin, smooth.

The leaves are eaten raw in salad or cooked as spinach. The fruit is sweet and can be eaten raw or used in jellies.

Sandy or gravelly roadsides, waste places, river bars.

AK YT

Chenopodium album

LAMB'S-QUARTERS

Annual herb from a taproot. **Flowers** greenish, small, inconspicuous, in leaf axils and sessile in irregular spikes at ends of stems. **Stems** erect (to 3 feet), stout, branched. **Leaves** alternate, broadly oval to lanceolate, the lower leaves are somewhat toothed, gray-green on underside.

Often cooked as greens.

Weedy on roadsides, waste areas.

AK | YT

11

OLEG KOSTERIN

OLEG KOSTERIN

IWAN SOBOLIEW

Allium schoenoprasum

WILD CHIVES

Perennial herb from an egg-shaped, scaly bulb. **Flowers** bright lavender, purple-striped, in a large, rounded, terminal head. **Stems** erect (6 inches), solitary, coarse, hollow. **Leaves** long slender, fleshy, hollow, flattish and onion-like, with characteristic onion odor.

The leaves are eaten in early spring, the bulbs in summer and fall.

Shores, streambanks, meadows.

AK YT

ALFRED COOK

COLE WOLF

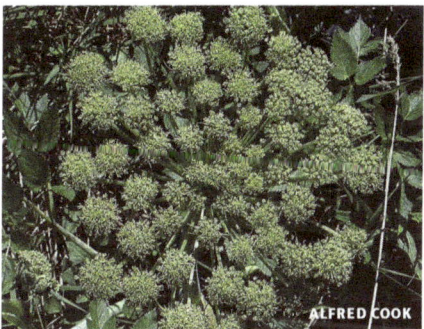
ALFRED COOK

Angelica lucida

SEACOAST ANGELICA

Stout perennial herb from a large taproot.
Flowers white, petals five, tiny, in a large,
almost flat, umbel at top of stalk. **Stems**
erect (up to 4 feet), coarse, hollow, shiny,
smooth. **Leaves** large, 3-parted, toothed,
shiny dark-green.

The juicy, hollow stems have a strong
taste but are eaten raw or cooked with fish.

Meadows, riverbanks, coastal areas.

AK YT

13 ▪

MATT BERGER

JASON GRANT

LAURALASKA66

Bupleurum americanum

AMERICAN THOROW-WAX

Annual herb. **Flowers** yellow, very tiny, a dozen or more in a flat, button-like cluster on a one-inch pedicel. A large group of these, in turn, form a large, flattened umbel. **Stems** erect (often 18 inches). **Leaves** long, narrow, simple, markedly veined; basal leaves pointed, stem leaves less so, and clasping, with a group of tiny leaves at base of umbel.

Meadows, woods; dry, rocky slopes and floodplains.

AK YT

■ 14

BARBARA BANFIELD

BARBARA BANFIELD

HENRIK KIBAK

EMMA READER-LEE

Cicuta douglasii

WESTERN WATER-HEMLOCK

Stout perennial herb from a taproot or cluster of tuberous roots. **Flowers** white to green-tinged, in a large umbel. **Stems** tall (to about 3 feet). **Leaves** divided 1-3 times, into lanceolate segments, these sharply pointed and toothed; lateral veins ending at base of the teeth.

Similar to *Cicuta virosa* in all respects (including the chambered taproot) except that the leaflets are broader.

Highly poisonous.

Marshes, streambanks, shores.

AK YT

STANISLAV MURASHKIN

VALERIA KOVALEVA

MARINA SADYKOVA

Cicuta virosa

WATER-HEMLOCK

SYNONYM *Cicuta mackenzieana*

Stout perennial herb from a taproot or cluster of tuberous roots. **Flowers** white, a number in a flat umbel, this is, in turn, a part of a much larger umbel; petals five, small. **Stems** erect (to 2 feet), stout, fleshy, hollow, from a hollow root. **Leaves** pinnately compound, segments slender, narrow, pointed, grass-like, very finely toothed.

Root chambered with horizontal partitions (visible when root cut lengthwise); when the root is cut, a yellow, oily liquid is also visible; highly poisonous.

Marshes, lakeshores, streambanks.

AK YT

ALFRED COOK

JASON GRANT

JASON GRANT

Cnidium cnidiifolium

DAWSON HEMLOCK-PARSLEY

SYNONYM *Conioselenum cnidiifolium*
Perennial herb. **Flowers** yellowish white, tiny, in small umbels on a one-inch stem; these are, in turn, part of a larger terminal umbel. **Stems** erect (to 3 feet), hollow. **Leaves** large, 3-times pinnate, attractive, lacy; each segment is pointed.
Poisonous.

Wet meadows, gravelly slopes, riverbanks.

AK **YT**

SUE CARNAHAN

GIANTCICADA

Heracleum maximum

COW-PARSNIP, WILD CELERY

Large perennial herb. **Flowers** white, tiny, 5-petaled, in a very large, flat, compound umbel. **Stems** erect (to 8 feet), grooved, hollow, branched; the coarse, dry stalks of the previous year are seen in mountain meadows in spring. **Leaves** enormous, maple-shaped, compound, serrate; near the flower umbels there are narrow, leafy-bracts.

The hairs on stems and leaves can be very irritating and lead to itching and rashes.

The marrow is eaten raw and the root boiled by the natives. Stems have a strong odor of celery and, when peeled, can be eaten raw; the roots are also edible when cooked; the plant contains sugar and tastes much like licorice.

Woods, moist slopes, streambanks, alpine meadows.

AK **YT**

■ 18

TATYANA PETRENKO

INGVILD RISKA

BENOIT RENAUD

Ligusticum hultenii

BEACH LOVAGE

SYNONYM *Ligusticum scoticum*

Perennial herb from thick taproot. **Flowers** pinkish white, very small, on short pedicels in large terminal umbels; petals five. **Stems** erect (to 2½ feet), smooth, stout, reddish, branched from a heavy rootstock; aromatic. **Leaves** broadly ovate, ternately compound, with 3 glossy green, much divided, toothed; leaflets on a long petiole.

Leaves and young stems eaten raw or cooked with fish.

Coastal beaches.

AK

ROB FOSTER

VALERII GLAZUNOV

MICHAEL NEWLON

Calla palustris

WATER ARUM

Perennial aquatic herb from a long, creeping rhizome. **Flowers** (and spathe) white (slightly greenish), calla-like, with a long point and a center of clustered green drupes; these turn red later in season. **Stems** erect, very fleshy. **Leaves** heart-shaped, broad, fleshy, on petioles but clasping.

Entire plant, especially the berries, poisonous, and although the toxins are neutralized by boiling or drying, eating this plant cannot be recommended.

Shallow water of bogs, ponds and streams.

AK YT

BRUCE KIRCHOFF

BRUCE KIRCHOFF

Oplopanax horridus

DEVIL'S-CLUB

Tall, deciduous shrub. **Flowers** greenish white, tiny, inconspicuous, in a large, branched, fleshy spike; followed in August by a large cluster of bright red berries. **Stems** erect (to about 6 feet), branched, stout, spiny. **Leaves** enormous, palmately lobed, veins and petioles prickly.

The flowers are very attractive to bees. Although the berries are considered toxic, many traditional medicinal uses have been made of this plant, a relative of ginseng.

Coastal areas; moist woods, rocky slopes; colonies form an almost impenetrable thicket.

AK YT

MARTINE LAPOINTE

TREELOGICAL

CALEB CATTO

Maianthemum stellatum

STARRY FALSE SOLOMON'S-SEAL

SYNONYM *Smilacina stellata*
Perennial herb from a slender, pale rhizome. **Flowers** white, small, star-shaped in a dense, terminal raceme; followed by inconspicuous berries. **Stems** graceful, slender (about 9 inches), very leafy, from a stout rootstock. **Leaves** lanceolate, broad, pointed, sessile, wide at stem end.

Flowering in late-May in the Matanuska Valley and nearby low-elevation areas.

Meadows, tidal flats, wet places.

AK YT

ANDREJUS GAIDAMAVIČIUS

BOB MILLER

Achillea millefolium

COMMON YARROW

Perennial, aromatic herb. **Flower heads** with both disk and ray flowers; flowers white (occasionally pink), tiny, in flat, branched, terminal corymbs. **Stems** erect (6–24 inches), hairy, often branched, gray-green, leafy. **Leaves** attractive, finely-cut, fern-like, tansy odor, alternate, those on stem smaller and sessile; leaf forms variable.

One of the first flowers seen in June and July at the Alaska-Yukon border.

Long-used for a variety of ailments.

Common on roadsides, in open fields, dry woods, alpine slopes.

AK YT

23 ■

Antennaria monocephala

PYGMY PUSSYTOES

Perennial mat-forming herb. **Flowers** white, fuzzy; female heads with gray-green calyx, usually solitary. **Stems** erect, though sometimes curved (2 inches), a dwarf, with very tiny, alternate stem leaves; short off-sets from base; forms mats. **Leaves** tiny, spatulate, somewhat fuzzy, densely tufted at base of flower stem.

There are quite a few species of *Antennaria* in the region, and separating them can be a challenge.

Gravelly slopes in alpine or arctic tundra, heathlands.

AK **YT**

■ 24

JOHN BREW

NATHAN SARLES

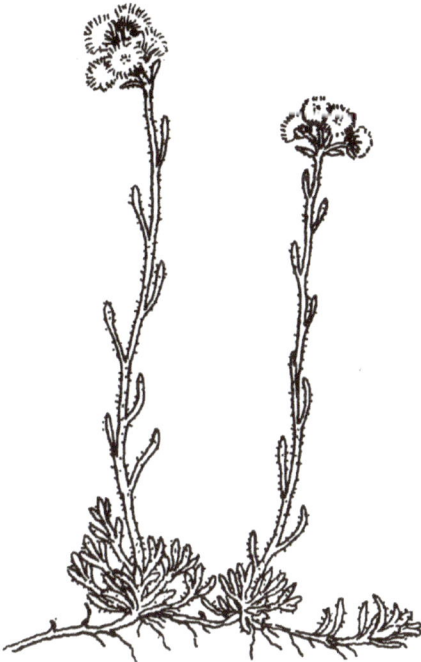

JACK BINDERNAGEL

Antennaria pulvinata

CUSHION PUSSYTOES

Perennial mat-forming herb. **Flowers** white, in small, soft fuzzy heads, 3-6 in a group terminal on stem. **Stems** erect (3–5 inches), hairy. **Leaves** grayish, basal ones oblanceolate and tufted; a number of stem leaves are small, alternate, with broad tips.
Open woods, dry alpine slopes.

AK YT

25 ■

LUKE PADON

P HOLROYD

JACOB REHAGE

Antennaria rosea

ROSY PUSSYTOES

Perennial mat-forming herb. **Flowers** pink, soft, fuzzy; female heads nodding, small, often a dozen in terminal group. **Stems** erect (to 10 inches), gray-green, with tiny, alternate stem leaves. **Leaves** small, narrow, pointed, gray-green woolly, chiefly in a basal tuft.

Alpine slopes, open woods, floodplains.

AK YT

VALERIA KOVALEVA

PAVEL SMIRNOV

KRZYSZTOF ZIARNEK

KRZYSZTOF ZIARNEK

Arctanthemum arcticum

ARCTIC DAISY

Perennial herb from a creeping rhizome or woody base. **Flower heads** with both disk and ray flowers; heads solitary; ray flowers white, disk flowers yellow. **Stems** erect (to 12 inches), single to several, unbranched, glabrous or sparsely woolly-hairy above. **Basal leaves** palmately lobed waxy-covered or green; **stem leaves** alternate, reduced upwards, the uppermost entire.

Marshes, tidal flats, wet meadows beaches.

AK YT

INGVILD RISKA

SERGEY GOLUBEV

HENRIK KIBAK

Arnica angustifolia

ALPINE ARNICA

SYNONYM *Arnica alpina*
Perennial herb, usually with one large terminal flower and two smaller ones from first leaf axils. **Flower heads** with both disk and ray flowers, rays deep-yellow. **Stems** erect (to 9 inches), hairy, seldom branched. **Leaves** long, slender, lanceolate, untoothed, somewhat hairy, in pairs on stem (2–3 pairs), sessile.

Open woods, arctic and alpine tundra.

AK YT

ZACK ABBEY

SHAAN AROESTE

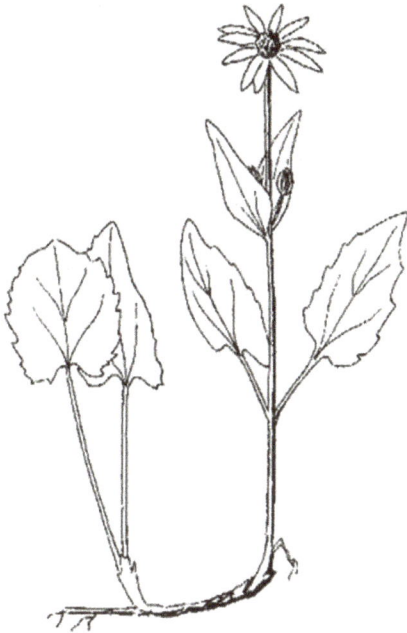

MACHAUT₂

Arnica cordifolia

HEART-LEAF ARNICA

Perennial herb from a long, branching rhizome, with a terminal flower and sometimes a smaller pair of flowers from upper leaf axils. **Flower heads** with both disk and ray flowers, yellow, large, white woolly on calyx. **Stems** erect (6–18 inches), slightly hairy. **Leaves** lanceolate, pointed but broad and heart-shaped at base, 2–3 pairs, mostly basal; hairy.

Woods.

AK YT

29

MATT MUIR

ERIC KNIGHT

MATT MUIR

Arnica griscomii

SNOW ARNICA

SYNONYM *Arnica louiseana*
Perennial herb. **Flower heads** with both
disk and ray flowers, pale yellow, usually
solitary, nodding, large. **Stems** erect (about
10 inches), solitary, hairy above. **Leaves**
abruptly pointed, very shallowly toothed, in
pairs, appearing more leafy than other
arnicas.

Arctic and alpine tundra, open woods.

AK YT

SIMONE

MATT BERGER

SHAAN AROESTE

Arnica lanceolata

LANCE-LEAF ARNICA

SYNONYM *Arnica amplexicaulis*

Perennial herb from creeping rhizomes, with a terminal flower and others in pairs from leaf axils. **Flower heads** with both disk and ray flowers, deep-yellow, large. **Stems** erect, tall (to 18–24 inches), substantial, only branched in inflorescence. **Leaves** lanceolate, pointed, in pairs; leaves on stem are small, sessile, lower leaves larger and finely toothed.

Moist woods, mountain slopes.

AK YT

LINDSEY SALMONSON

BROOKE SMITH

JONATHAN CURLEY

Arnica latifolia

BROAD-LEAF ARNICA

Perennial herb from creeping rhizomes.
Flower heads with both disk and ray flowers, deep-yellow, as many as five. **Stems**
erect, very slender, often tall. **Leaves** broad,
tending to heart-shaped but pointed, a tiny
pair of leaves sessile on stem; lower leaves
with petioles and toothed, with pronounced
veins.

Open woods, alpine meadows.

AK YT

JACK BINDERNAGEL

JACK BINDERNAGEL

AERIN JACOB

AMEET MANDAVIA

Arnica lessingii

LESSING'S ARNICA

Perennial herb from a rhizome. **Flower heads** with both disk and ray flowers, solitary, usually nodding; ray flowers yellow, conspicuously toothed; disk flowers yellow; anthers purple. **Stems** solitary (to 12 inches), sometimes branched above. **Basal leaves** smaller than stem leaves, often deciduous by flowering time; **stem leaves** mostly 3–4, very low on the stem, lanceolate to elliptic, entire to toothed.

Arctic and alpine tundra, heathlands.

AK YT

33 ■

MARTINE LAPOINTE

ANDREY ZHARKIKH

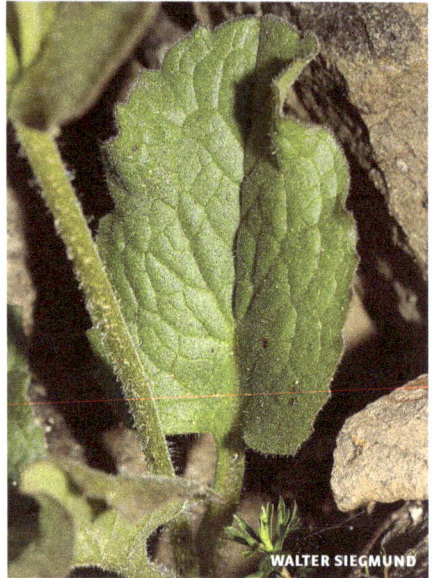

WALTER SIEGMUND

Arnica ovata

STICKY-LEAF ARNICA

SYNONYM *Arnica diversifolia*

Perennial herb, from a rhizome. **Flower heads** with both disk and ray flowers, butter-yellow, usually 1-4, the bases hairy and often glandular; ray flowers 12-15, inconspicuously toothed. **Stems** erect (to about 12 inches), solitary or occasionally a few clustered together, sparsely long-hairy and often glandular. **Basal leaves** smaller than stem leaves and often deciduous by flowering time; **stem leaves** opposite, 2-4 pairs, uppermost ones reduced.

Open woods.

AK YT

VALERIA KOVALEVA

MARIA KHOREVA

PAVEL SMIRNOV

Artemisia canadensis

NORTHERN WORMWOOD

SYNONYM *Artemisia borealis*
Perennial (sometimes biennial) herb from a taproot, scarcely aromatic. **Flowers** greenish yellow, small, round, button-like, scattered on single stalk. **Stems** erect (to 1 foot), thick, stout. **Leaves** much dissected, mostly basal, gray-silky.

Arctic and alpine tundra, heathlands, open woods.

AK YT

35 ■

MATT BERGER

SAM KIESCHNICK

MICHELLE W

Artemisia dracunculus

LINEAR-LEAF WORMWOOD

Perennial herb from a stout rhizome, slightly to strongly aromatic. **Flowers** grayish yellow-green, tiny, very numerous in a tall, pointed spike. **Stems** erect (to 2–3 feet), stout, almost woody near base, branched. **Leaves** long, slender, pointed (willow-like) with noticeable midveins.

Found in south-central Alaska and southern Yukon on dry rocky slopes, roadsides.

AK YT

JARED LINCENBERG

ERIC LAMB

TONY KM

Artemisia frigida

PRAIRIE SAGEWORT

Perennial herb from a woody crown. **Flowers** greenish, small and inconspicuous, on a dense spike. **Stems** spreading (to 10 inches), silvery gray, slender. **Leaves** silver-gray, finely cut into delicate, linear divisions, fan-shaped in general outline.

The smoke from its burning leaves can help repel mosquitoes.

Dry rocky slopes, highway cut-banks.

AK YT

Artemisia kruhsiana

ALASKA WORMWOOD

SYNONYM *Artemisia alaskana*
Perennial herb from a more or less woody crown. **Flowers** grayish brown, small, round, sparsely arranged on stalk. **Stems** erect, but branched and low-growing, silvery-gray. **Lower leaves** dissected into linear divisions, these blunt-ended, broader, and more coarsely cut than in *Artemisia frigida,* but silvery-gray also; narrow pointed leaves intermixed with the flowers.

Sand and gravel bars, floodplains, rocky ledges.

AK YT

ERIC LAMB

JASON HOLLINGER

Artemisia norvegica

ARCTIC WORMWOOD

SYNONYM *Artemisia arctica*

Perennial herb from a short, branched base. **Flowerheads** greenish yellow, small, round, on a tall, branched, terminal spike. **Stems** erect (to 2 feet), stout, branched, glabrous. **Leaves** green, glabrous on upper-side (vs. silvery in some of our other *Artemisia* species), 2–3 times pinnate, lobes long and pointed; lower leaves large, on slender petioles, with small leaves in the flower heads.

Arctic and alpine tundra, heathlands.

AK YT

39 ■

ALEKSEY BAUSHEV

VALERII GLAZUNOV

QUINTEN WIEGERSMA

Artemisia tilesii

TILESIUS' WORMWOOD

Perennial, aromatic herb from a rhizome. **Flowers** greenish, very small and inconspicuous but numerous, on a very tall, branched spike. **Stems** erect (up to 4 feet), sometimes branched, often red. **Basal leaves** large, broad, dissected and deeply toothed, sessile; many small, entire leaves in inflorescence; leaves smooth, green on upper sides, grayish velvety on underside.

Arctic and alpine tundra, heathlands, roadsides.

AK YT

■ 40

JOHN POW...

ANDERS HASTINGS

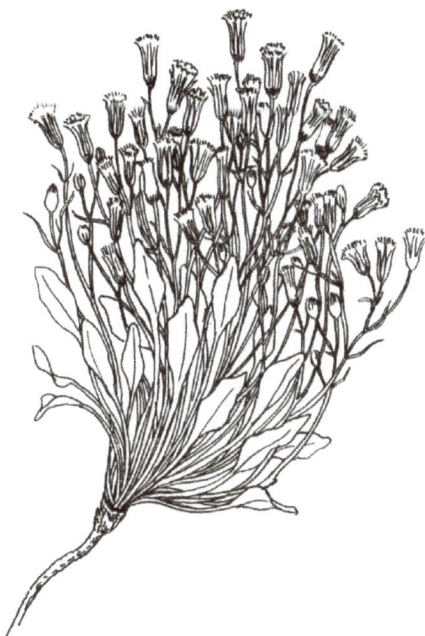

Askellia pygmaea

DWARF HAWK'S-BEARD

SYNONYM *Crepis nana*
Perennial herb from a taproot and woody base. **Flowerheads** of yellow ray flowers only, small, dandelion-like, not fully opening; phyllaries a deep olive-green. **Stems** erect (to 6 inches), often 50 or more from one large taproot; sap milky, brownish green. **Leaves** with small, broad blade, slightly toothed, brownish green, on long petiole, chiefly basal.

The plant varies greatly in size, often a crowded small bunch or tussock of flowers.

Sand or gravel river bars, talus slopes, roadsides.

AK YT

41

ANNA MITROSHENKOVA

CALEB CATTO

PHILIP SCHARF

THIERRY ARBAULT

Aster alpinus

ALPINE ASTER

Perennial herb from a woody base or rhizome. **Flowerheads** with both disk and ray flowers, solitary; ray flowers white (sometimes lavender); disk flowers yellow. **Stems** erect to ascending (to 12 inches), shortly gray-hairy. **Basal leaves** spoon-shaped, more or less rounded at tip; **stem leaves** becoming smaller upwards on stem.

Grassy slopes, sandy flats, rocky alpine tundra.

AK YT

ANNA MITROSHENKOVA

IAN ADAMS

ERIC LAMB

Crepis tectorum

NARROW-LEAF HAWK'S-BEARD

Introduced annual herb from a short tap-root. **Flowerheads** of ray flowers only, several to many in a more or less flat-topped head; rays yellow. **Stems** erect (to about 18 inches), solitary, branched, glabrous or hairy, with milky juice. **Basal leaves** lance-olate or oblanceolate, entire to toothed or pinnately parted, often soon deciduous; **stem leaves** clasping, mostly linear or nearly so.

A weed of roadsides, river bars, waste places.

AK YT

ANASTASIIA MERKULOVA

ANNA MITROSHENKOVA

Erigeron acris

BITTER FLEABANE

Biennial or perennial herb. **Flowerheads** with both disk and ray flowers; terminal on branched stems, several in a group; rays purplish pink, the phyllaries are sometimes purplish. **Stems** erect (to 2 feet), much branched, slightly hairy, with numerous small, pointed leaves. **Leaves** narrow, oblanceolate, pointed, smooth-edged, somewhat hairy.

Flowering in mid-July and later. A number of other *Erigeron* species are present in the region, often growing on roadsides or on gravelly soils.

Sandy roadsides, gravel bars, shores, open woods.

AK YT

Erigeron compositus

DWARF MOUNTAIN FLEABANE

Perennial herb from a taproot. **Flowerheads** with both disk and ray flowers, solitary, on a stem rising well above basal leaves; ray flowers white. **Stems** erect (to 6 inches), with few, tiny linear, leaves. **Leaves** very small, 3–5 lobed, finely segmented, grayish fuzzy, basal.

A tufted, dense-growing, dwarfed plant. Open slopes, rocky places, lakeshores.

Another common species is **Tufted Fleabane** (*Erigeron caespitosus*), found in dry, gravelly open areas of the region.

AK | **YT**

JACK BINDERNAGEL

J STRAKA

JACK BINDERNAGEL

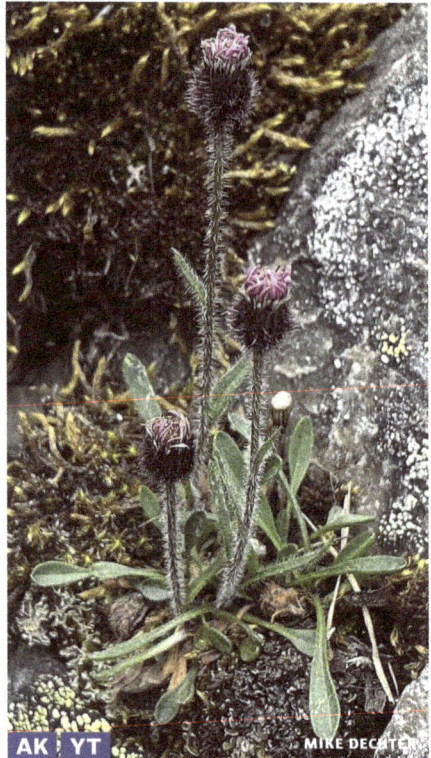

AK YT

MIKE DECOTEAU

Erigeron humilis

LOW FLEABANE

Perennial herb from a short taproot or a short woody base. **Flowerheads** with both disk and ray flowers; solitary at end of stems; ray flowers white to purplish. **Stems** to 10 inches, purplish, long-hairy. **Basal leaves** oblanceolate; **stem leaves** reduced upwards, linear.

Arctic and alpine tundra, soils often gravelly.

SIMONE

SIMONE

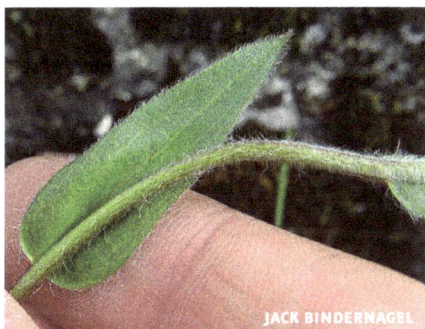

JACK BINDERNAGEL

Erigeron peregrinus

SUBALPINE FLEABANE, WANDERING DAISY

Perennial herb from a rhizome or short, stout stem-base. **Flowerheads** with both disk and ray flowers, solitary and fairly large; ray flowers purple, with yellow center. **Stems** erect (3-18 inches), fuzzy, leafy. **Leaves** lanceolate, long, slender, pointed, alternate on stem; basal leaves blunt.

Subalpine and alpine meadows, open woods.

AK YT

47

PETER CASEY

J STRAKA

Eurybia sibirica

SIBERIAN WOOD-ASTER

SYNONYM *Aster sibiricus*
Perennial herb from a slender rhizome.
Flowerheads with both disk and ray flowers, 1-4 heads on a stem; ray flowers lavender to purple, with dark disk flowers at center. **Stems** erect (6-10 inches), branched, woolly, leafy. **Leaves** lanceolate, pointed, somewhat broad, slightly toothed, woolly, lower leaves petioled, upper are sessile.

A mid-season flower, very variable in size, number of flowers, etc.

Sandy roadsides, meadows, streambanks, rocky slopes.

AK YT

STEVE MATSON

MATT BERGER

Hieracium triste

WOOLLY HAWKWEED

SYNONYM *Hieracium gracile*
Perennial herb from a short, stout rhizome.
Flowerheads of yellow ray flowers only;
these few, small, dandelion-like, in a terminal group; the involucre is black-hairy.
Stems erect (to 12 inches), slender, with a
few finely cut leaves. **Leaves** mostly basal,
long, spoon-shaped, slightly toothed, on
long petioles.

There are other similar species of *Hieracium,* both native and introduced, present in the region.

Alpine meadows, streambanks, talus
slopes, roadsides.

AK YT

49 ∎

BOB MILLER

MATT BERGER

STUART FRASER

Leucanthemum vulgare

OX-EYE DAISY

Introduced perennial herb from a creeping rhizome. **Flower heads** with both disk and ray flowers, solitary on long stalk; ray flowers white, with yellow disk flowers at center. **Stems** erect, slender (to 3 feet), usually unbranched. **Leaves** basal ones spatulate-ovate, with petioles; stem leaves small, sessile, coarsely toothed, dark green.

Weed of waste places; common along roads south of the Alaska Range.

AK | YT

JENNY SAITO

BOB MILLER

MICHAEL NEWLON

Matricaria discoidea

PINEAPPLE-WEED

SYNONYM *Matricaria suaveolens*
Annual herb, pineapple-scented. **Flower heads** with disk flowers only, these greenish yellow, tiny, in a cone (and looking like a small pineapple); rays absent. **Stems** erect (to 8–10 inches), much branched. **Leaves** 2-3 times pinnate, lobes narrow and delicate, fern-like, aromatic when crushed.

The flowerheads are sometimes used to make a flavorful tea.

Waste places.

AK YT

51

ILYA RUDENKO

ILYA RUDENKO

ILYA RUDENKO

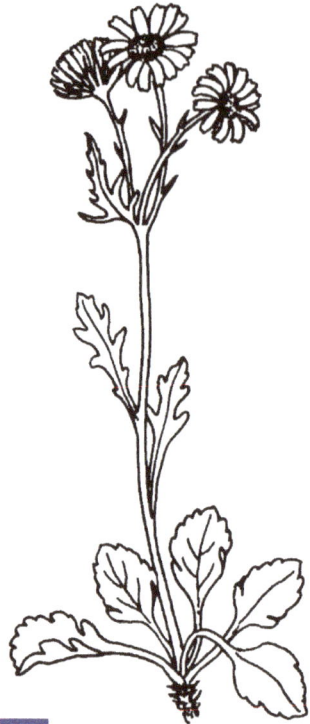

Packera heterophylla

DWARF ARCTIC GROUNDSEL

SYNONYM *Senecio residifolius*
Perennial herb from a short rhizome. **Flower heads** with both disk and ray flowers; ray flowers deep-yellow, phyllaries often purplish. **Stems** erect (4–8 inches), slender, solitary, purplish with tiny bracts near flower head and a few small stem leaves. **Basal leaves** nearly round, the leaves becoming longer and entire to coarsely toothed upward on stem, purplish.

Arctic and alpine tundra, heathlands.

AK YT

JACK BINDERNAGEL

JACK BINDERNAGEL

ROSACEAE_ROBERTS

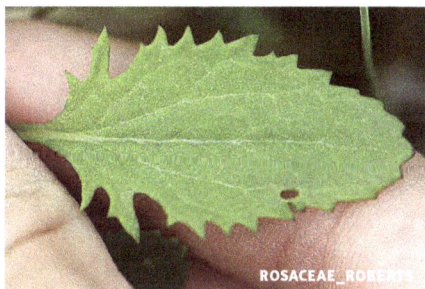

Packera pauciflora

ALPINE GROUNDSEL

SYNONYM *Senecio pauciflorus*

Perennial herb from a fibrous-rooted, woody base. **Flower heads** with disk flowers only (ray flowers absent), orange-yellow, on long stems, a few in an open, terminal group; phyllaries purplish. **Stems** erect (3–15 inches), solitary, with a few small, alternate leaves. **Basal leaves** ovate to nearly round on long petioles, thick, succulent; margins toothed.

Alpine meadows, open woods, shores.

AK | YT

53 ∎

ANNIE BÉLAIR

CALEB CATTO

Petasites frigidus var. *sagittatus*

ARROWLEAF SWEET COLT'S-FOOT, ARROWLEAF BUTTERBUR

SYNONYM *Petasites sagittatus*

Perennial herb from a creeping root. **Flowers** white when open, purplish pink in bud, in a large, loose cluster or corymb, followed by a large cluster of silky-white heads; the flowers appear before the leaves. **Stems** erect (6–15 inches), solitary, fleshy, woolly, with many pointed bract-like leaves. **Leaves** large (4–6 inches wide), broad, coarse, arrow-shaped, fleshy, slightly toothed, woolly on underside, on long petioles, basal, from the rhizome.

The similar *Petasites frigidus* var. *frigidus* is usually at higher elevations, and has a broader and more deeply cut leaf.

Bogs, wet meadows, tundra.

AK YT

ETHAN WRIGHT

ETHAN WRIGHT

JASON GRANT

Saussurea angustifolia

NARROW-LEAF SAW-WORT

Perennial herb from a rhizome. **Flower-heads** of disk flowers only, these royal-purple, not fully opening, in blackish, scaly-bracted cups, with several blossoms at top of stem, each on a long stalk. **Stems** erect (to 18 inches), rigid, usually purplish brown. **Leaves** lanceolate, long, narrow, pointed and very slightly toothed; with a few small leaves on flower stem but chiefly basal.

Bogs, open woods, meadows.

AK YT

55 ◼

MEGAN HERRMANN

ALAN COVINGTON

JACK BINDERNAGEL

Senecio lugens

BLACK-TIP GROUNDSEL

Perennial herb from a short, thick rhizome. **Flowerheads** with both disk and ray flowers, 5–10 in a fairly compact head; ray flowers yellow; the bracts of the flowers are black-tipped. **Stems** erect (15–18 inches), solitary, stout, ridged, woolly in young plants. **Leaves** lanceolate, long, pointed, with finely toothed edges; stem leaves small.

Tundra, bog margins.

AK YT

DMITRY IVANOV

TOBY V.

MARTINE LAPOINTE

Senecio pseudoarnica

SEASIDE RAGWORT

Perennial herb from a rhizome. **Flower-heads** with both disk and ray flowers, large, single to several on glabrous to woolly-hairy stalks; ray flowers yellow; disk flowers yellow; young flower buds white-woolly. **Stems** solitary (to 2 feet), simple or branched, glabrous below, woolly-hairy above. **Basal leaves** usually smaller than the stem leaves, deciduous by flowering time; **stem leaves** thick, toothed, woolly-hairy on both sides or the upper surface smooth.

Sandy beaches, dunes, tidal flats.

AK

JARED LINCENBERG

BRANDON CORDER

ANDERS HASTINGS

Senecio triangularis

ARROW-LEAF RAGWORT

Perennial herb from a fibrous-rooted, woody stem-base or rhizome. **Flower-heads** small, with both disk and ray flowers, in loose clusters at top of a tall stem; ray flowers yellow. **Stems** erect (to 3 feet), stout, weedy, very leafy, branched. **Leaves** lance-shaped, long, pointed, very evenly serrated edges, dark green, shining, a very attractive leaf and noticeable even before flowers bloom.

Blossoms in July and August.

Moist mountain meadows, open woods, bogs.

AK **YT**

GIANTCICADA

MARK POLLOCK

MATT BOWSER

AK YT

Solidago lepida

ELEGANT GOLDENROD

Perennial herb from a creeping rhizome. **Flowerheads** small, with both yellow disk and ray flowers; in a rather long, compact terminal head. **Stems** erect (12 inches or more), slender, solitary, leafy. **Leaves** oblanceolate, blunt, finely toothed, lower leaves have petioles almost as long as leaves.

Meadows, fields, open woods.

59 ■

RYAN SORRELLS

CHRIS FRIESEN

TODD BOLAND

Solidago multiradiata

NORTHERN GOLDENROD

Perennial herb from a short rhizome. **Flow-erheads** with small, yellow disk and ray flowers, usually in a dense terminal head, with scattered small heads in upper leaf axils. **Stems** erect (to 15 inches), usually single, somewhat leafy. **Leaves** long-oval, sharp pointed, alternate, on petioles, somewhat hairy, the smaller stem leaves are sessile.

Meadows, rocky woods, alpine tundra.

AK   YT

JUSTIN DONAHUE

DAN MACNEAL

ALAN PRATHER

Symphyotrichum boreale

NORTHERN BOG-ASTER

SYNONYM *Aster junceus*
Perennial herb from a slender rhizome.
Flowerheads with both disk and ray flowers, these small, several on a stem or solitary; ray flowers white, disk flowers yellow.
Stems erect (about 1 foot), often purple-tinged, hairy near flowers. **Leaves** lanceolate, linear, slightly toothed, sessile.

A late-season plant of bogs and other wet places.

AK **YT**

SUE CARNAHAN

TODD BOLAND

AK YT

STEVE MATSON

Taraxacum ceratophorum

Taraxacum

DANDELION

HORNED DANDELION

Nine species of *Taraxacum* are reported for Alaska and the Yukon; seven of which are considered native to the region (BONAP). The **Common Dandelion** (next page) is a familiar weed, and its young leaves are sometimes used as an early spring green. This and the native **Horned Dandelion** (this page) can be distinguished as follows:

Coarse weedy plants; outer bracts reflexed; inner involucral bracts usually swollen at tip .... Common Dandelion (*T. officinale*)
Plants smaller; outer bracts appressed or ascending; inner involucral bracts not swollen at tip   Horned Dandelion (*T. cerataphorum*)

Native perennial herb from a thick, often black, taproot. **Flowerheads** of yellow ray flowers only, single at end of a naked stem; inner involucral bracts usually swollen or with appendages at their tips ("horns"). **Stems** ascending to erect (to about 10 inches), solitary to several, simple, hollow, glabrous or sparsely long-hairy, exuding milky juice when broken. **Leaves** all basal, lanceolate to oblanceolate, usually pinnately lobed, the terminal lobe often wider than the others, tapering at the base to a winged petiole, glabrous or nearly so.

Tundra, meadows, rocky slopes; found throughout Alaska and the Yukon.

ANDREW SEBASTIAN

BARRY COTTAM

Taraxacum officinale

COMMON DANDELION

Introduced perennial herb from a thick, deep taproot; **Flowerheads** of yellow ray flowers only; these single at end of a naked stem; inner involucral bracts long-pointed, without appendages. **Stems** erect (to about 12 inches), solitary to several, simple, hollow, glabrous or sparsely long-hairy, with milky juice when broken. **Leaves** all basal, lanceolate to oblanceolate, usually pinnately lobed, tapering at the base to a winged petiole, glabrous or slightly hairy.

Roadsides, fields, yards, gardens, waste places.

AK YT

63 ■

NPS, JACOB W. FRANK

ALFRED COOK

ALFRED COOK

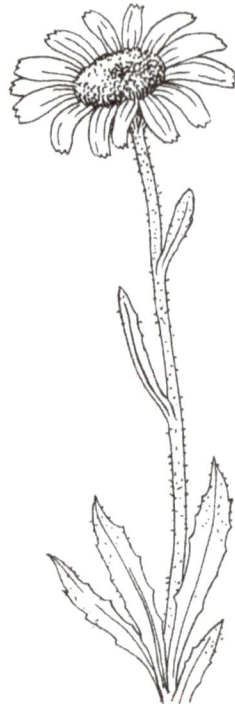

Tephroseris frigida

ARCTIC SENECIO

SYNONYM *Senecio atropurpeus*
Perennial herb from a rhizome. **Flower-heads** with both disk and ray flowers, solitary; ray flowers yellow, phyllaries often fuzzy brown. **Stems** erect (6–9 inches), with a few small, sessile leaves. **Leaves** oval, long, blunt-tipped, narrowing to the petiole, mostly basal, usually very woolly.

Moist meadows, arctic and alpine tundra.

AK YT

VALERII GLAZUNOV

VALERII GLAZUNOV

YURII BASOV

Tephroseris palustris

MARSH FLEABANE

SYNONYM *Senecio congestus*
Annual or biennial herb from a fibrous root.
Flowerheads with both disk and ray flow-ers, rather small, in small groups which make up a large, terminal cluster; ray flow-ers lemon-yellow. **Stems** erect (to 3 feet), thick, hollow, much-branched, hairy, a large, leafy plant. **Leaves** linear to oblance-olate, pointed, large, sessile and broad at base, very fleshy, very woolly.

The young leaves and stalks are consid-ered edible as salad greens.

Moist shores, streambanks, seeps, bogs.

AK   YT

MARTINE LAPOINTE

HADYNRMURRAY

LIAM STEELE

Tripleurospermum inodorum

SCENTLESS MAYWEED

SYNONYM *Matricaria inodora*

Introduced annual, biennial or sometimes perennial, scentless herb from a fibrous root. **Flowerheads** with both disk and ray flowers; ray flowers white, disk flowers yellow, the heads similar to the common ox-eye daisy. **Stems** erect (to 3 feet), much branched, glabrous. Leaves very finely pinnately dissected into linear segments; leaves not numerous.

Shores and waste places.

AK **YT**

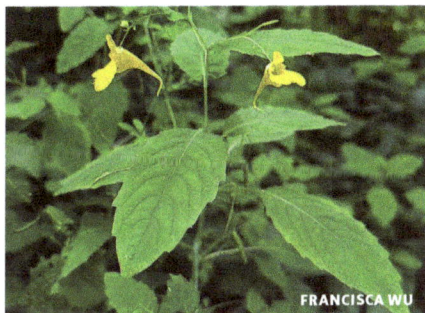

Impatiens noli-tangere

WESTERN TOUCH-ME-NOT, JEWEL-WEED

Annual succulent herb. **Flowers** yellow, dotted with brown, each with a long spur, on slender peduncles from upper leaf axils; followed by a succulent, light-green seed pod which can be snapped. **Stems** erect (12–18 inches), branched, tender, light green, almost transparent. **Leaves** broad, lanceolate, pointed, smooth, succulent.

Low elevations where wet; usually in semi-shade.

AK YT

67 ∎

ALLAN HARRIS

LAURALASKA66

LAURALASKA66

Eritrichium aretioides

ALPINE FORGET-ME-NOT

Tufted perennial herb. **Flowers** brilliant sky-blue, with a yellow eye, 1–2 blossoms on a stem; petals 5, tiny. **Stems** erect (about 1–1½ inches), gray-green and very fuzzy, rise from woody root. **Leaves** longish, sharp-pointed, very fuzzy, mostly in a very tightly bunched basal rosette; old leaves persisting.

Forms a rounded "pin cushion."

Arctic and alpine tundra in dry, sandy, rocky or gravelly places.

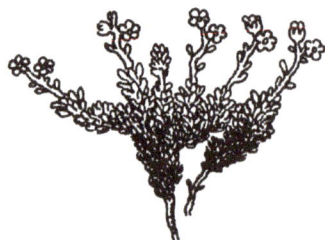

AK YT

Mertensia maritima

SEA LUNGWORT, OYSTERPLANT

Perennial herb from a taproot. **Flowers** bright blue, (pink in bud) very small, in terminal clusters; petals 5. **Stems** decumbent, trailing, mat-forming. **Leaves** broad-ovate, thick, fleshy, grayish-green, alternate.

A fleshy beach plant which grows in large circular mats on the sand. In the Yukon, only known from the shores of the Arctic Ocean.

Sandy coastal shores.

AK YT

ERIC LAMB

CALEB CATTO

Mertensia paniculata

TALL BLUEBELLS

Perennial herb from a taproot. **Flowers** brilliant blue (pink in bud and occasionally pink when fully open), bell-shaped, in long, drooping panicles; petals 5. **Stems** erect (8–24 inches), hairy, often several branches from one root. **Leaves** long, broad, large, lanceolate, on petioles, sparsely gray-hairy on both sides.

One of the earliest, most beautiful, and most widely distributed (at least in driving areas) of the region's wildflowers; may be seen from late-May through June, July, and into August.

Woods, meadows, gravel bars, streambanks.

AK YT

CALEB CATTO

CALEB CATTO

ILYA RUDENKO

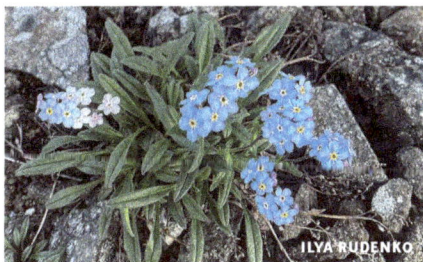

Myosotis asiatica

ASIAN FORGET-ME-NOT

SYNONYM *Myosotis alpestris*
Perennial herb from fibrous roots. **Flowers** sky-blue (occasionally pink) with yellow 'eye'; usually in a terminal panicle, though in some seasons found in a small, compact, terminal cluster; petals 5. **Stems** erect (to 10 inches), often branched, hairy, with tiny stem leaves. **Leaves** lanceolate, long, pointed, hairy, opposite, gray-green; basal leaves spatulate and on petioles.

Alaska's official state flower.

Alpine and subalpine meadows, thickets, rocky slopes.

AK | YT

71

HOMER D. HOUSE

BRASSICACEAE
Mustard Family

This family has a large number of genera (42) and species (over 100) present in Alaska and the Yukon. Many of these are not native to the region and are often weedy. In general, our members of this family can be described as follows:

Flowers white, light lavender, or yellow; petals 4; stamens 6; usually in loose, terminal clusters, followed by two-valved seed pods; these either nearly round (silicle) or long and slender (silique). **Stems** erect, many grow to about 6–15 inches. **Leaves** variable: small species tend to have entire leaves; large species tend to have pinnate or lyrate leaves.

Twelve of the more common Mustard family species of the region are described on the following pages.

Arabidopsis lyrata (RIGHT)

LYRE-LEAF ROCKCRESS

SYNONYM *Arabis lyrata*
Biennial or short-lived perennial herb. **Flowers** in racemes of 5–15; petals white to pale pink. **Stems** 1-several, simple or branched, to about 10 inches tall, glabrous throughout or sparsely stiff-hairy near base. **Basal leaves** in a distinct rosette, spoon-shaped, simple and entire or with a few large teeth; **stem leaves** few, not ear-like at base, entire. **Fruit** an upright silique.

The leaves are edible.

Tundra, woods.

CHARLIE

AK

■ 72

RYAN DONNELLY

VICTOR BARDASHEV

AK | **YT**

Barbarea orthoceras

YELLOW-ROCKET

Biennial (sometimes perennial) herb from a taproot. **Flowers** in terminal racemes or racemes in lower leaf axils; petals pale yellow. **Stems** erect (about 12 inches), stiff, angled, branched. **Basal leaves** pinnately lobed, with 1–5 pairs of lateral lobes, the terminal lobe the largest, entire or irregularly toothed; **lowermost stem leaves** with 2–10 pairs of lateral lobes, **upper stem leaves** often clasping the stem. **Fruit** an erect to somewhat spreading silique.

Moist streambanks, seeps, beaches, roadsides.

AK | **YT**

Brassica rapa

FIELD-MUSTARD

Introduced annual herb from a taproot. **Flowers** in terminal clusters; petals yellow. **Stems** simple to freely branched (about 12 inches), glabrous or sparsely hairy, glaucous. **Basal leaves** pinnately cleft with 2–4 lateral lobes and the terminal lobe the largest; **lower stem leaves** similar to the basal but ear-like at base and clasping or sessile, **upper stem leaves** narrowly ovate, nearly entire. **Fruit** an upright to spreading silique.

Fields, roadsides, disturbed places.

Y. LIU

SAM KIESCHNICK

JOSE CARR

Capsella bursa-pastoris

SHEPHERD'S-PURSE

Annual herb from a taproot. **Flowers** many in a raceme; petals white, with a distinct stalked base. **Stems** simple to branched (about 12 inches), with simple and starlike hairs. **Basal leaves** in rosettes, oblanceolate, nearly entire to pinnately lobed; **stem leaves** clasping stem, with earlike lobes at the base. **Fruit** a triangular silicle.

Fields, roadsides, waste places.

AK YT

ILYA FILIPPOV

ER-BIRDS

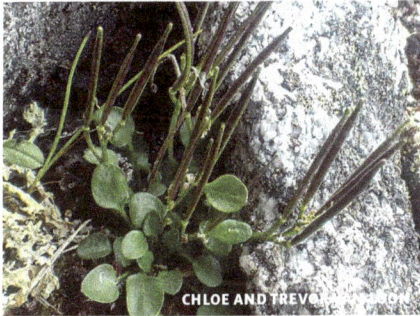

CHLOE AND TREVOR VAN LOON

AK **YT**

Cardamine bellidifolia

ALPINE BITTERCRESS

More or less tufted, dwarf, perennial herb from a taproot. **Flowers** few in an umbel-like raceme; petals white. **Stems** several (to about 4 inches), few-leaved, glabrous. **Basal leaves** in rosettes, thick, fleshy, entire or shallowly lobed; **stem leaves** absent or several, reduced in size. **Fruit** an erect silique.

Arctic and alpine tundra, often where gravelly or rocky.

AK **YT**

Cardamine polemonioides

CUCKOO-BITTERCRESS

SYNONYM *Cardamine pratensis*
Perennial herb from a rhizome. **Flowers** in a terminal cluster or raceme; petals pinkish lavender. **Stems** erect (6–12 inches), slender. **Leaves** pinnate (with 8–15 leaflets); basal leaves have broad leaflets, stem leaves narrow, linear, fern-like. **Fruit** an erect silique.

Tundra, heath, woods.

75 ■

NPS, JACOB W. FRANK

LAURALASKA66

CHERYL MCCLEARY-CATALANO

Cardamine purpurea

PURPLE BITTERCRESS

Perennial herb from a rhizome. **Flowers** in terminal clusters; petals pink, pink-purple, or white. **Stem** short, 2–4 inches tall. **Leaves** pinnately divided, with a broad leaflet at tip and narrow leaflets toward the base. **Fruit** an erect silique.

The young leaves are edible.

Moist alpine meadows, wet tundra.

AK YT

Draba aurea

GOLDEN WHITLOW-GRASS

Perennial herb from a taproot. **Flowers** in several to many in racemes; petals pale- to deep-yellow. **Stems** erect or decumbent at base (to about 18 inches), simple or branched, hairy. **Basal leaves** oblanceolate, entire or coarsely toothed; **stem leaves** 10–20; leaves densely hairy, lower leaf surfaces with mainly star-like hairs.

There are nearly 50 species of *Draba* reported for the region, and they can be quite difficult to separate from one another.

Gravelly soils, rock outcrops, low to high elevations.

AK **YT**

JASON GRANT

JASON GRANT

VALERIA KOVALEVA

Draba borealis

NORTHERN WHITLOW-GRASS

Loosely tufted perennial herb from a taproot. **Flowers** several to many in racemes; petals white to cream. **Stems** erect or decumbent at base (to about 18 inches), branched, hairy. **Basal leaves** oblanceolate, toothed or entire; **stem leaves** 3–6; leaves hairy with 4- to 6-rayed, star-like hairs and also often simple or branched hairs.

Alpine tundra, heathlands, open woods.

AK | YT

MICHELLE NORCÉIDE

MARTINE LAPOINTE

BENOÎT RENAUD

BOBO-X

Erysimum cheiranthoides

WORM-SEED WALLFLOWER

Introduced annual or biennial herb from a taproot. **Flowers** in racemes; petals pale-yellow. **Stems** simple or branched (to 3 feet), leafy, sparsely hairy with 2-pronged hairs. **Basal leaves** absent; **stem leaves** linear to lanceolate, entire or minutely toothed, finely hairy with 3-pronged hairs. **Fruit** an upright silique.

Weed of disturbed places.

AK YT

INGVILD RISKA

DAVID MCCORQUODALE

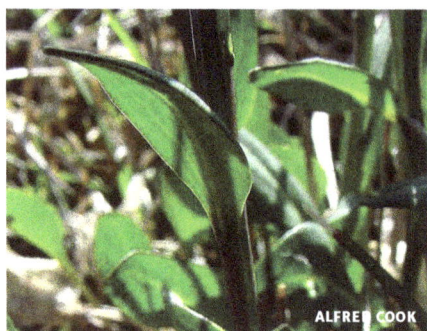

ALFRED COOK

Eutrema edwardsii

EDWARD'S MOCK WALLFLOWER

Perennial herb from a slender taproot. **Flowers** 3–20 in racemes; petals white or cream. **Stems** ascending to erect (to 18 inches), glabrous. **Basal leaves** ovate or elliptic, margins entire; **stem leaves** reduced upwards. **Fruit** (right) an upright, purplish silique.

Arctic and alpine tundra, talus slopes, heathlands.

AK YT   NINA NESTEROVA

MEGAN HERRMANN

DAN VICKERS

Parrya nudicaulis

NAKED-STEM WALLFLOWER

Tufted perennial herb. **Flowers** pinkish-lavender, on short pedicels in an open, terminal raceme; petals 4, small. **Stems** erect (to 8 inches), stout, leafless. **Leaves** long-oval, pointed, on petioles, some are slightly toothed, all basal.

Somewhat variable in size of flower and form of leaf; grows in the open, at high altitudes, often with *Anemone narcissiflora*.

Sometimes called 'Little Cabbages,' as the leaves and the long, thick root are edible.

Arctic and alpine tundra, heathlands.

AK YT

81

NATHAN AARON

STANISLAV MURASHKIN

NUUJAKA

Rorippa palustris

BOG YELLOWCRESS

Annual, biennial, or short-lived perennial herb from a slender taproot. **Flowers** in a raceme; petals light-yellow. **Stems** erect (to 2–3 feet), simple to much branched from base, glabrous to stiff-hairy. **Leaves** oblong, irregularly toothed or divided, with slightly clasping, ear-like lobes at base, long-pointed at tip, petioles short or absent; glabrous or stiff-hairy.

Roadsides, open hillsides, disturbed places.

AK **YT**

JACK BINDERNAGEL

NPS, JACOB W. FRANK

CALEB CATTO

Campanula lasiocarpa

MOUNTAIN HAREBELL

Perennial herb from a slender rhizome. **Flowers** deep-purple, solitary, shaped like a large, upturned bell; corolla lobes somewhat pointed. **Stems** erect (6–8 inches), hairy. **Leaves** long-oval, wider at tip, pointed, somewhat toothed, hairy.

A beautiful alpine species, the bell is large for the size of the small tuft of leaves.

Rocky alpine slopes and ridges, open woods, muskegs.

AK YT

83

IAN ADAMS

IAN ADAMS

CALEB CATTO

Campanula rotundifolia

ALASKAN BELLFLOWER

Perennial herb from a taproot or slender rhizome. **Flower** a purple bell, rather large, 1–2 on stem, slightly drooping. **Stems** erect (about 8 inches), slender, wiry, smooth, sometimes branched. **Stem leaves** grass-like, fine, alternate, sessile; **basal leaves** nearly round, on long petioles.

Gravelly roadsides, grassy slopes, rock outcrops.

AK YT

MY-LAN LE

KIM HANSEN

EERO KOSKINEN

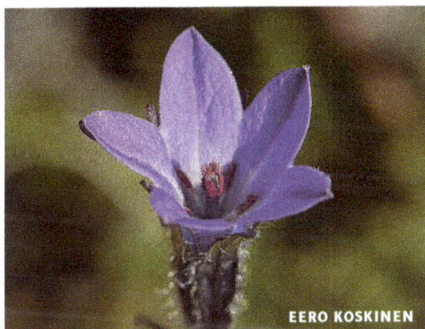

Melanocalyx uniflora

ARCTIC-HAREBELL

SYNONYM *Campanula uniflora*
Perennial herb from a taproot or slender rhizome. **Flowers** a purple bell, medium-size, solitary, slightly nodding. **Stems** erect (to 7 inches), slender, glabrous. **Leaves** several on stem, narrow, lanceolate and slightly toothed; most leaves in a basal rosette; these are wider, pointed, somewhat toothed, on petioles; all are glabrous.

Gravelly tundra and heath.

AK YT

BRIAN GRATWICKE

RYAN HODNETT

JAMES ST. JOHN

Linnaea borealis

TWINFLOWER

Evergreen semi-woody herb or subshrub.
Flowers pink, tiny, in a trumpet-shaped
bloom; in pairs on a slender, erect, bare,
branched stem from a woody stem; petals 5.
Stems trailing, long, slender. **Leaves** small,
round, in opposite pairs, evergreen.

Moist woods, thickets and slopes, usually
in semi-shade.

AK **YT**

ILYA RUDENKO

ILYA FILIPPOV

ILYA RUDENKO

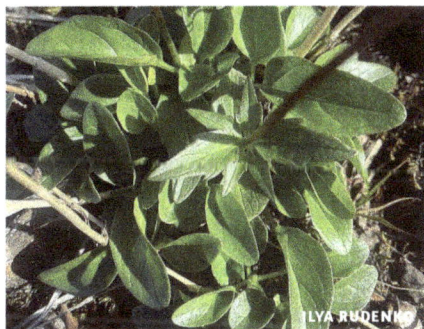

Valeriana capitata

CLUSTERED VALERIAN

Perennial herb. **Flowers** white (sometimes pink in bud), tiny; female flowers in rather small, loose, terminal heads. **Stems** erect (to 12 inches), often branched, hollow, smooth, with a few small sessile leaves; more slender than in *Valeriana sitchensis*. **Leaves** 3- to 5-lobed, toothed, surface smooth, in opposite pairs, the central lobe often very broad and round tipped.

Heathlands, tundra, moist woods.

AK | YT

87

THAYNE TUASON

TIMOTHY MCNITT

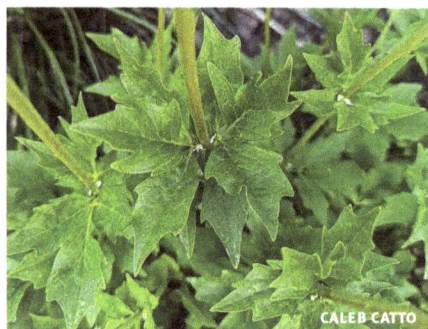

CALEB CATTO

Valeriana sitchensis

SITKA VALERIAN

Perennial herb from a stout rhizome. **Flowers** white (pinkish in bud), fragrant; pistillate flowers tiny in rather large, flattened terminal heads, often with tiny heads from upper leaf axils. **Stems** erect (to 2 feet), hollow, smooth, rather coarse; sometimes branched. **Leaves** 3-5-lobed, with coarsely, irregularly toothed margins; upper stem leaves smaller.

Moist meadows, heathlands, woods.

AK YT

CRICKET RASPET

ARCHER SILVERMAN

TODD_BOLAND

Cerastium arvense

FIELD CHICKWEED

Tufted perennial, forming loose mats, plants glabrous to glandular-hairy. **Flowers** 3–5 or more in an open inflorescence; petals 5, white, twice as long as the sepals, deeply bi-lobed; sepals 5, glandular-hairy; stamens 10; styles 5. **Flowering stems** to about 12 inches tall. **Leaves** opposite, linear to narrowly lanceolate; stem leaves often with bundles of secondary leaves in their axils.

Alpine tundra, heath, rocky hillsides, meadows.

AK YT

JACK BINDERNAGEL

TODD BOLAND

BOB WALKER

Cerastium beeringianum

BERING MOUSE-EAR CHICKWEED

Tufted perennial, glandular-hairy with spreading hairs. **Flowers** solitary or 2-5 in an open cluster; petals 5, white, 1.5–2 times as long as the sepals; sepals 5, often purplish, notched; stamens 10; styles 5. **Flowering stems** to about 10 inches tall. **Leaves** opposite, narrowly oblong, without sterile shoots or secondary leaves in the axils.

Arctic and alpine tundra, heath, open slopes.

AK YT

Cherleria arctica

ARCTIC STITCHWORT

SYNONYM *Minuartia arctica*
Perennial herb from a taproot and branching base; forming loose mats. **Flowers** white, or often pinkish-tinged,; single at ends of short stems, well-raised above the plant cushion; petals 5, not much longer than the sepals. **Stems** slender (about 2 inches long), leafy, glandular-hairy. **Leaves** small, linear.

Dry, rocky and gravelly alpine tundra.

AK YT

RAINERBURKARD

MARTINE LAPOINTE

HKNUETTEL

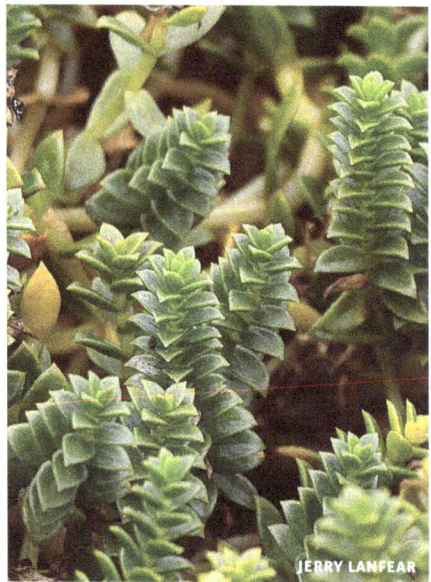

JERRY LANFEAR

Honckenya peploides

SEASIDE SANDPLANT

SYNONYM *Arenaria peploides*
Succulent perennial herb from a deep tap-root and slender rhizomes; forming mats. **Flowers** single or few from the upper leaf axils; petals 5, greenish-white. **Stems** numerous, trailing, usually freely branching, glabrous; flowering stems prostrate to erect. **Stem leaves** opposite, from lanceolate to ovate, fleshy, yellowish green, glabrous, often with axillary shoots; **basal leaves** absent.

Sandy beaches along the coasts.

AK YT

ATTILA OLÁH

NINA HOUSE

CONNY KLEIN

Silene acaulis

MOSS CAMPION, CUSHION-PINK

Perennial herb from a woody root. **Flowers** deep pink to purplish, small, flattened, long-throated, solitary on short stems; petals 5. **Stems** bearing flowers erect, less than 6 inches; other stems branched; very densely hairy. **Leaves** lanceolate, linear, narrow, pointed, grayish fuzzy, moss-like.

Forms small, round, domed mats.

Arctic and alpine tundra, heathlands.

AK YT

Stellaria

CHICKWEED, STARWORT, STITCHWORT

Twelve species are reported from the region (BONAP); one, *Stellaria media,* is considered introduced from Eurasia. Following is a general description:

Flowers white, small, petals five, deeply-notched; usually solitary or in small, terminal groups, on stems from upper leaf axils. **Stems** sometimes lax, often prostrate, branched. **Leaves** narrow, slender, usually pointed, opposite and sessile or short-stalked.

Three common species are described below. **Long-Stalk Starwort** (*Stellaria longipes*) is illustrated (Photo, line drawing, RIGHT).

LONG-STALK STARWORT | JACK BINDERNAGEL

Stellaria crassifolia

FLESHY STITCHWORT

Perennial, mat-forming herb from slender rhizomes. **Flowers** usually single from the leaf axils, or occasionally several flowers in an open cluster; petals 5, white, deeply 2-cleft. **Stems** decumbent to erect, many, branched, very slender. **Leaves** opposite, narrow, unstalked.

Muskegs, lakeshores, meadows; soils moist. Alaska, Yukon. (*not illus.*)

Stellaria longipes

LONG-STALK STARWORT

Perennial herb from slender rhizomes, often mat-forming. **Flowers** single to several in an open head; petals 5, white, slightly longer than the sepals. **Stems** glabrous, 4-angled. **Leaves** opposite, sessile, stiff, glaucous, narrow, usually glabrous.

Streambanks, shores, sandy slopes. Alaska, Yukon.

Stellaria media

COMMON CHICKWEED

Introduced annual herb (sometimes over-wintering in mild areas), taprooted. **Flowers** in small leafy clusters at ends of stems; petals 5, white deeply notched, **Stems** weak, trailing. **Leaves** opposite, broadly elliptic, with a petiole.

A common weed of disturbed places. Alaska, Yukon. (*not illus.*)

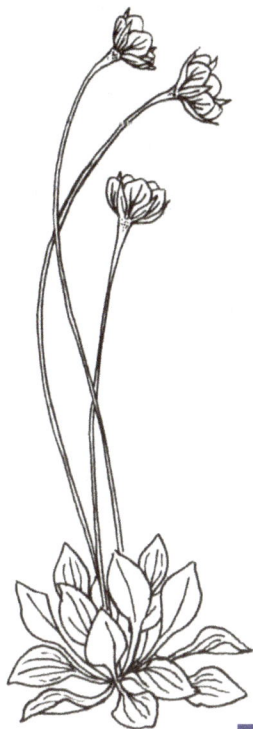

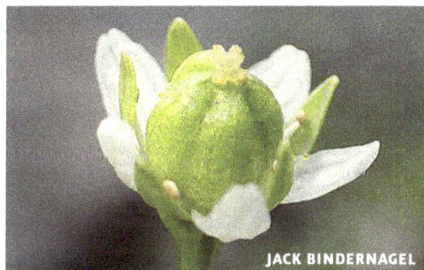

Parnassia kotzebuei

KOTZEBUE'S GRASS-OF-PARNASSUS

Perennial herb from a short rootstock. **Flowers** white, solitary; petals 5, rounded, somewhat smaller than those of *Parnassia palustris*. **Stems** erect (usually less than 6 inches), slender, stem leaves absent. **Leaves** wide-rounded, narrow at tip, small, all basal.

A much smaller plant than *Parnassia palustris* and found at higher elevations.

Wet alpine meadows, streambanks, tundra.

AK | YT

95

ATTILA OLÁH

ANNA MITROSHENKOVA

Parnassia palustris

MARSH GRASS-OF-PARNASSUS

Perennial herb from a short rootstock. **Flowers** white, solitary; petals 5, large, rounded, longer than sepals. **Stems** erect (3–12 inches), slender, stiff, usually one small leaf. **Leaves** heart-shaped, small, on short petioles, almost all basal, appearing small for height of flower stems.

Parnassia greets the traveler at the Yukon border in July, and is one of the first wildflowers seen along the Glenn Highway as it approaches the first of the Matanuska Valley farms.

Roadside ditches, wet meadows, tundra.

AK YT

Cornus canadensis

BUNCHBERRY

Low, trailing perennial herb from a rhizome. **Flowers** (bracts) white (occasionally pink-tinged), four, petal-like; the drupes mature into bright orange or red pithy berries. **Stems** erect (4–8 inches), from a slender rootstock. **Leaves** large, broadly oval, pointed, short-petioled, noticeably veined, chiefly in a whorl-like formation at top of stem (often a pair of small, sessile leaves below the whorl).

The berries are edible when mixed with a more tart variety.

Moist woods, tundra, subalpine slopes.
Cornus alba, the **Red-Osier Dogwood**, a red-stemmed, woody shrub with white petal-like bracts, followed by white berries, and reaching about 8 feet, is found in moist woods in Alaska and mostly the southern half of the Yukon.

AK YT

CALEB CATTO

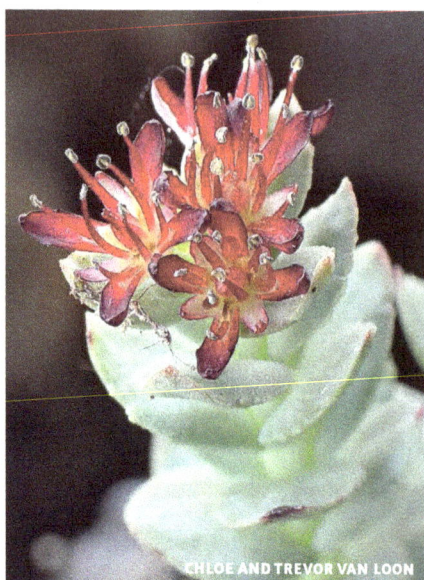

CHLOE AND TREVOR VAN LOON

Rhodiola integrifolia

ROSEROOT

SYNONYM *Sedum rosea*
Perennial herb from a thick, branched rhizome; mat-forming. Flowers dark reddish purple, in a flat, very dense, terminal corymb; petals 4, tiny. Stems erect (to 12 inches), fleshy, gray-green, leafy, from a fleshy, rose-scented rootstock. Leaves oblanceolate, pointed, sessile, gray-green, fleshy, numerous all down stem.

The young leaves and roots are edible, raw or cooked. The cut root smells somewhat like a rose.

Arctic and alpine tundra, heath.

AK YT

■ 98

BENOIT RENAUD

CALEB CATTO

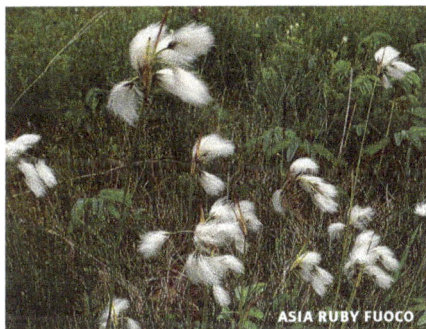

ASIA RUBY FUOCO

Eriophorum angustifolium

TALL COTTONGRASS

Perennial grass-like herb. **Heads** tan to creamy, a number in a terminal cluster or umbel. **Stems** erect, angular, (1–2 feet tall). **Leaves** (leaf blades) long, flat in middle, with thickened sharp point.

Lower stems and roots edible.

Common plant of bogs, muskeg, shallow ponds; low to high elevations.

AK   YT

99 ■

SUE CARNAHAN

Eriophorum scheuchzeri

WHITE COTTONGRASS

Perennial grass-like herb from creeping rhizomes, forming colonies. **Heads** white, medium-sized, oval, soft, solitary. **Stems** erect (to 20 inches), slender, without bracts. **Leaves** few, mostly basal.

Used in the past as a wound dressing and for stuffing pillows.

Shores, muskeg, wet meadows, roadside ditches.

The three species described here can be separated as follows. Note, however, that there are about 10 different cottongrass species reported for the region.

1 Spikes several, drooping or clustered, subtended by 1 or 2 leafy bracts . . . .
. . . . *E. angustifolium*
1 Spikes solitary, not subtended by leafy bracts 2
2 Plants spreading by stolons . . . .
. . . . *E. scheuchzeri*
2 Plants densely tufted . . . . *E. vaginatum*

AK YT

■ 100

ROB FOSTER

ROB FOSTER

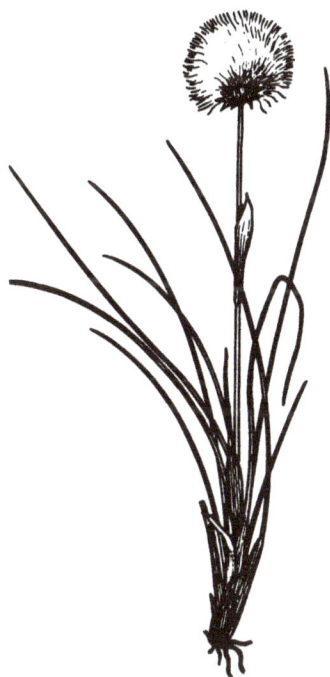

ROB FOSTER

Eriophorum vaginatum

TUSSOCK COTTONGRASS

Perennial grass-like herb, forming clumps. **Heads** white, large, fluffy, solitary at ends of stems. **Stems** erect (to about 18 inches), many in a clump. **Stem leaves** 1–3, slender, folded.

Bogs, marshes, wet meadows at mid- to high-elevations.

AK YT

101 ∎

TODD BOLAND

TODD BOLAND

ERIC LAMB

STRAKA

Diapensia lapponica

PINCUSHION-PLANT, LAPLAND DIAPENSIA

Dwarf evergreen shrub, often forming large mats. **Flowers** white, bell-like, uplifted; centers yellow; pinkish when old; petals 5. flower stems erect (1–2 inches), tinged with red. **Trailing stems** woody, much-branched. **Leaves** narrow, obovate, tiny, thick, evergreen, curved, in a dense basal tuft.

Arctic and alpine tundra, heathlands.

AK YT

CALEB CATTO

CALEB CATTO

CALEB CATTO

Elaeagnus commutata

SILVERBERRY, WOLF WILLOW

Deciduous shrub from a strong rhizome. **Flowers** yellow inside, silvery outside, fragrant, usually 2–3 in leaf axils; petals 4, small and inconspicuous; followed by a mealy, edible berry. **Stems** erect (to 8–10 feet); bark silvery and brown-hairy (like shiny copper), smooth. **Leaves** broad-oval, with pointed tip, smooth-edged, thick, gray-silvery on both sides.

The silvery berry is edible but tasteless. The large seeds have been used as beads.

Dry slopes, river bars.

AK **YT**

103 ∎

CALEB CATTO

CALEB CATTO

JACK BINDERNAGEL

Shepherdia canadensis

RUSSET BUFFALO-BERRY, SOAPBERRY

Deciduous shrub, with male and female flowers borne on separate plants. **Flowers** pale yellow, small and inconspicuous, in small clusters in leaf axils; followed by a red berry. **Stems** erect (3–6 feet), branched, hairy, a woody shrub. **Leaves** oval, smooth-edged, opposite, shiny green above and silvery on back.

Blossoms early, with berries by mid-July.

Native people beat the berries with sugar and water to make a frothy dish. The berries are a favorite bear food.

Sandy streambanks, shores, open woods.

AK YT

DIETER SCHULTEN

MARTINE LAPOINTE

CHLOE & TREVOR VAN LOON

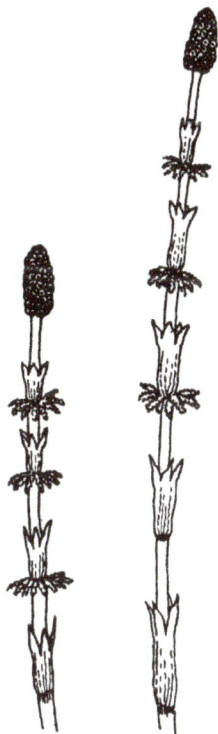

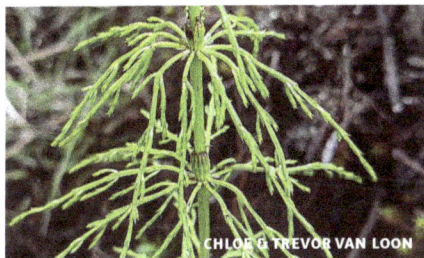

Equisetum sylvaticum

WOODLAND HORSETAIL

Fern-like perennial from a smooth rhizome.
Stems erect (4–15 inches), hollow, ridged,
with terminal bud in a loose, toothed
sheath. **Leaves** tiny, fern-like, in whorls
around the stem. The brown spore-bearing
stems appear very early (these becoming
green), followed by the green sterile shoots.

Other horsetails are present in the region, some producing their spores at the
end of the vegetative stem rather than a
separate fertile stem.

Lowland forests to the subalpine,
meadows.

AK YT

105 ■

MARTINE LAPOINTE

MAURICE RAYMOND

TODD BOLAND

Andromeda polifolia

BOG-ROSEMARY

Small evergreen shrub. **Flowers** (and flower stems) pink, bell-shaped (but almost closed), nodding, on long pedicels in terminal umbel; sepals a darker rose color. **Stems** erect (to 1 foot), woody, wiry, brownish, somewhat branched, a low shrub. **Leaves** narrow, pointed, leathery, evergreen, margins rolled, lighter green underneath.

Poisonous.

Bogs, swamps, wet tundra.

AK **YT**

CALEB CATTO

JARED SHORMA

MATT PELIKAN

Arctostaphylos uva-ursi

BEARBERRY, KINNIKINNICK

Prostrate shrub, sometimes forming mats. **Flowers** pink, small, nodding, bell-shaped, 5–12 in a terminal cluster; followed by bright red, attractive, but mealy and tasteless berries. **Stems** creeping, 3–6 inches, woody, the branches very flexible. **Leaves** oval with wide, blunt tips, tiny, evergreen, leathery, with smooth margins, on petioles; persisting through the winter.

Dry woods, exposed places in sand or gravel.

AK YT

107 ■

MARTINE LAPOINTE

ERIN MCKITTRICK

AKR

Arctous alpina

BLACK ALPINE BEARBERRY

SYNONYM *Arctostaphylos alpina*
Prostrate shrub with rhizomatous stems. **Flowers** greenish white, small, bell-shaped, 2–3 in a terminal group, followed by bluish black fruit. **Stems** decumbent, bark woody, often forming large mats. **Leaves** dark green, willow-like but more rounded, attractively net-veined, margins finely toothed, on petioles; with scattered hairs on the petioles and margins of lower portion of leaf blades. **Fruit** black, edible but lacking flavor.

Leaves turn bright red in the fall; old leaves often persisting, with plants flowering before the new leaves develop (see photo, upper right).

Gravelly alpine tundra, generally at higher elevations than the otherwise very similar (apart from the black vs. red berries) *Arctous rubra.*

AK | YT

■ 108

JASON GRANT

CALEB CATTO

JACK BINDERNAGEL

RED BEARBERRY

The related *Arctous rubra*, **Red Bearberry** (photos, this page), with juicy red berries, is found throughout the region in open conifer woods, bogs, moist meadows, tundra; usually at lower elevations than *Arctous alpina*. Other distinguishing features are the presence of hairs on the petioles and leaf margins of *Arctous alpine* (absent in *A. rubra*), and the larger leaves of *A. rubra*. The leaves of *Arctous alpina* persist for several years; those of *A. rubra* do not and when they are shed, leave areas of leafless stem.

AK YT

109

SUE CARNAHAN

DAVE

AIVA NORINGSETH

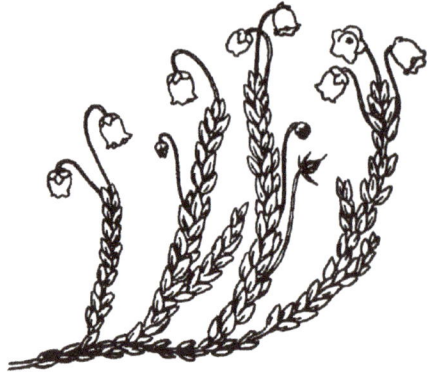

Cassiope tetragona

ARCTIC BELL-HEATHER

Dwarf mat-forming shrub. **Flowers** white, open, waxy, bell-shaped, nodding; usually single on a slender, erect pedicel. **Stems** creeping, prostrate. **Leaves** evergreen, oblong, very fine, narrow, hard and scalelike, grooved, clasping stem, overlapping each other.

Arctic and alpine tundra, heathlands.

AK YT

STEVEN LAMONDE

CHRISTINE YOUNG

Chamaedaphne calyculata

LEATHERLEAF

Shrub. **Flowers** white, urn-shaped, in one-sided leafy terminal racemes. **Stems** erect (to about 2 feet), branching, covered with short white hairs, sometimes also scaly. **Leaves** evergreen (turning brown in winter), alternate, leathery, oblanceolate to elliptic, finely sharp-toothed, margins flat or rolled under, scaly-hairy.

Bogs, muskegs, lake margins.

AK YT

CONNY KLEIN

ROBERT FLOGAUS-FAUST

DARMOZRAC

Empetrum nigrum

BLACK CROWBERRY

Mat-forming evergreen shrub. **Flowers** pinkish, small and inconspicuous, scattered in leaf axils, blooming early; followed by a juicy, seedy, black berry. **Stems** trailing, low, much-branched, a woody vine. **Leaves** linear, needle-like, evergreen, denser at stem ends.

Berries usually formed by mid-June, frequently used in pies or jellies.

Bogs, swamps, heathlands, from low to high elevations.

AK YT

JACK BINDERNAGEL

ALEXANDRIA WENNINGER

KATHERINE BAIRD

NOLAN EXE

Harrimanella stelleriana

ALASKA BELL-HEATHER, MOSS-PLANT

SYNONYM *Cassiope stelleriana*

Dwarf mat-forming shrub. **Flowers** white, bell-shaped, solitary, nodding, on a slender erect pedicel. **Stems** decumbent (to 5 inches), leafy. **Leaves** small, needle-like, soft, evergreen, thick, overlapping on stem.

May form large clumps; plants have a strong odor.

Arctic and alpine tundra, moist woods near the coast; uncommon in the Yukon.

AK **YT**

113 ■

THIERRY ARBAULT

ER-BIRDS

Kalmia procumbens

ALPINE AZALEA

SYNONYM *Loiseleuria procumbens*
Dwarf, mat-forming shrub. **Flowers** pink to
rose, bell-like but open, in terminal clusters;
petals 6, very small, pointed. **Stems** creeping (2–4 inches), much branched. **Leaves**
oval-rounded, very small, stiff, evergreen,
closely set like a moss.

Arctic and alpine tundra, heathlands;
often growing with lichens.

AK YT

TODD BOLAND

ANDREW BAZDYREV

Moneses uniflora

SINGLE-DELIGHT, ONE-FLOWER WINTERGREEN

SYNONYM *Pyrola uniflora*

Perennial, slightly woody herb from slender, rhizome-like root. **Flowers** white, solitary, nodding, terminal, fragrant; petals five, pointed, waxy with rolled edges; stamens noticeable, with a long protruding anther. **Stems** erect (3–6 inches), leafless, from a slender rootstock. **Leaves** ovate to round, margins very finely toothed, thin, on short petioles, in a basal cluster.

AK **YT**

Moist, mossy, shaded woods.

MARTINE LAPOINTE

TODD BOLAND

TODD BOLAND

Orthilia secunda

SIDEBELLS, ONE-SIDED WINTERGREEN

SYNONYM *Pyrola secunda*

Perennial, slightly woody herb from a rhizome, often forming colonies. **Flowers** greenish white, bell-like, with a projecting straight style, up to 20 flowers on one side of the stem. **Stems** erect (to 6 inches), rather slender, pinkish, with 2 tiny bracts. **Leaves** roundish-oval and somewhat pointed, on short petioles, in a basal rosette of 5–6 small, shiny leaves.

Moist, shady woods; arctic and alpine tundra.

AK YT

J STRAKA

MAREK

AERIN JACOB

Phyllodoce glanduliflora

YELLOW MOUNTAIN-HEATH

Low, matted shrub. **Flowers** yellow, bell-shaped, nodding on a slender pedicel, a few in a terminal group. **Stems** prostrate (about 6 inches); a low, branching, woody-stemmed shrub. **Leaves** linear, round-ended, very small, leathery, evergreen, crowded on stem.

Dry mountain slopes, heathlands.

AK YT

117 ■

CALEB CATTO

TODD BOLAND

CALEB CATTO

Pyrola asarifolia

PINK WINTERGREEN

Perennial herb from a rhizome. **Flowers** deep-pink, bell-shaped with curved styles and deep-colored anthers, numbering about 20 along a single stem; petals rather thin in texture. **Stems** erect (6–8 inches), slender, with many dry, pointed bracts clasping stem. **Leaves** nearly round, thick, leathery, on long petioles, in a basal group of 5 or 6.

Moist woods, alpine meadows.

AK **YT**

EVAN GRIMES

WENDY MCCRADY

WENDY MCCRADY

Pyrola chlorantha

GREEN-FLOWER WINTERGREEN

Perennial herb from a slender rhizome.
Flowers greenish white, bell-like, with
short, curved style; 6–8 flowers grouped on
end of stem. **Stems** erect (5–6 inches),
rather stout. **Leaves** rounded, few, small,
basal; petioles often longer than leaf is
wide.

Woods.

AK YT

119 ■

Pyrola grandiflora

ARCTIC WINTERGREEN

Perennial herb from a slender rhizome. **Flowers** creamy-white (pinkish late in season), open ended, with yellow anthers and a long curved style; petals fleshy-thick, veined a darker shade; many fragrant flowers on a scape. **Stems** erect (4–8 inches), with a few dry bracts. **Leaves** rounded, thick, leathery, on long petioles, usually 3–4 in a basal rosette.

Shaded woods, arctic and alpine tundra.

AK YT

DMITRY IVANOV

NATALIA KAZAKOVA

MARINA DAVLETSHINA

Pyrola minor

LESSER WINTERGREEN

Perennial herb from a slender rhizome.
Flowers white to very light pink; rather flat
bell-shaped, small, almost closed, with
short, straight styles; with 6–17 flowers spirally arranged at top of stem. **Stems** erect
(3–12 inches), naked except for one bract.
Leaves broad, long-oval, thick, on stout
petioles, all basal.

Shaded woods, alpine slopes.

AK YT

121 ■

MARTINE LAPOINTE

SARAH RICHER

RYAN SEALY

Rhododendron groenlandicum

BOG LABRADOR-TEA

SYNONYM *Ledum groenlandicum*
Upright shrub. **Flowers** white, in a showy cluster at stem end; petals 5, small. **Stems** erect (1–3 feet); a much-branched, woody shrub. **Leaves** thick, narrow, about an inch long, blunt-tipped, with rolled edge; upper side smooth, green; underside gray to red, woolly.

Aromatic when crushed, and the dried leaves have long been used for tea.

Muskegs, bogs, wet woods, alpine slopes.

AK YT

PC SMITH

DANILOVA VALERIA

Rhododendron lapponicum

LAPLAND AZALEA

Dwarf, mat-forming shrub. **Flowers** bright magenta to deep-red, each on a short stalk, with 3–4 in a terminal group; flowers large for size of total plant. **Stems** prostrate (to 8 inches), low-growing, branched, hugging the ground in a mat; a somewhat scaly, woody shrub. **Leaves** oval, round-ended, small, thick, evergreen, brownish on backs, in whorls at ends of stems.

Arctic and alpine tundra, open woods.

AK YT

123

STEVE ANSELL

ALEX WILD

STEVE JOHN MARTIN

Rhododendron menziesii

FOOL'S-HUCKLEBERRY

SYNONYM *Menziesia ferruginea*
Straggly shrub, with somewhat skunky
odor. **Flowers** orange-pink, bell-like, on
long, curved pedicels, slightly fragrant, in
small groups at stem ends; petals 4. **Stems**
erect (3–4 feet); a woody shrub, branched.
Leaves oblanceolate, with a short, narrow
tip, of a somewhat bluish green, chiefly in a
terminal group or cluster.

Moist woods, often in partial shade. **AK**

Rhododendron tomentosum

MARSH LABRADOR-TEA

SYNONYM *Ledum palustre*
Shrub. **Flowers** white, on slender pedicels in a small terminal head; petals 5, small. **Stems** almost creeping (6-8 inches), woody, rather slender. **Leaves** thick, narrower than in *Rhododendron groenlandicum*, with noticeable midrib, dark green on top, reddish underneath; margins inrolled; leaves aromatic when crushed.

For the casual observer, there is very little difference between this species and *Rhododendron groenlandicum*; in general *Rhododendron tomentosum* grows at somewhat higher elevations, its leaves are narrower, and the total plant and flower cluster are smaller.

Long used to make a flavorful tea.
Bogs, heathlands.

AK YT

125 ■

JROSSMUNRO

RYAN DURAND

NOAH HOW

Vaccinium cespitosum

DWARF BILBERRY

Spreading, matted shrub. **Flowers** bell-shaped, bright pink, solitary in terminal leaf axils; followed by a sweet blue berry with a whitish bloom. **Stems** low (about 8 inches), branched, brown, woody. **Leaves** small, narrowly ovate, brownish when young, finely serrate, thin, developing well after the flowers. **Fruit** a round berry, light blue to blackish blue with a waxy bloom; sweet.

Bogs, wet meadows, alpine tundra; from low to high elevations.

AK YT

■ 126

YASTOKOZ

KATERINA GRISHINA

NIKITA TIUNOV

ODENWAELDER

Vaccinium oxycoccus

BOG CRANBERRY

Small, creeping shrub. **Flowers** bright pink, bell-shaped with four tiny petals, often with recurved margins, 1–4 in a terminal group; followed by a tart, translucent red berry. **Stems** lax (about 4 inches), thread-like; a dwarfed plant. **Leaves** minute, short, pointed, leathery, evergreen, sparse, lighter on underside, margins inrolled. **Fruit** a red berry, edible but tart.

Sphagnum bogs, swamps.

AK **YT**

MARTINE LAPOINTE

NIKITA TIUNOV

ROB FOSTER

Vaccinium uliginosum

BOG BILBERRY

Small woody shrub. **Flowers** light pink or white tipped with pink, bell-shaped, from 1–4 in axils from old wood; hanging below the leaves which tend to grow vertically; followed by a blue-black berry with white bloom. **Stems** erect (to 2 feet), much-branched, bark shreddy. **Leaves** oval, small, thick, lighter underneath. **Fruit** a globe-shaped berry, blue with a waxy bloom; edible and sweet

A much-used fruit in Alaska, with many families gathering large quantities for winter use.

Bogs, muskegs, swamps, tundra.

AK YT

STEVE ANSELL

PETER ZACHUFF

MARKUS HORRER

Vaccinium vitis-idaea

LINGONBERRY, MOUNTAIN-CRANBERRY

Low, mat-forming shrub. **Flowers** delicate pink, open bell-shaped, in a cluster at stem ends; followed by a small, red berry with the same tart taste as the cultivated cranberry. **Stems** creeping (4–8 inches), branched, slender, very leafy, woody. **Leaves** blunt oval, very small, leathery, evergreen, smooth, shiny, with slightly turned margins, very numerous on stem. **Fruit** a globe-shaped, bright red berry; edible but acidic.

May be confused with **Bearberry** (*Arctostaphylos uva-ursi*), but Lingonberry leaves are oval with notched tips, have a prominent midvein, and are rounded at both ends. Bearberry has longer leaves that taper towards the stem, and its berries are orange-red rather than the burgundy-red of Lingonberry.

Used in Alaska in a many different ways including baking and jellies. Berries typically ripen in early September, with the flavor improving after a frost.

Most often in moist, open woods; also on bog hummocks, heathlands, tundra.

AK YT

129 ■

MIKKO LEHIKOINEN

MATTHIAS BUCK

MATTHIAS BUCK

Astragalus alpinus

ALPINE MILK-VETCH

Low mat-forming perennial herb from a taproot and rhizomes. **Flowers** pea-like, white with purple edges, to pure purple or lavender; in a rather rounded, open head or raceme. **Stems** partially decumbent, branched, the flower stems erect, slender, naked, rising from leaf axils. **Leaves** odd-pinnate (more than 13 leaflets); leaflets small, slender, blunt tipped, whitish on underside.

Sandy slopes, tundra, river beds, roadsides.

AK YT

MARIA_L

ALEJANDRO DELGADO

Astragalus umbellatus

TUNDRA MILK-VETCH

SYNONYM *Astragalus frigidus*
Perennial herb, from a buried base with
rhizome-like branches. **Flowers** pea-like,
yellow to cream color, 5–15 in a rather compact raceme. **Stems** erect (4–20 inches).
Flower stalks stout, solitary. **Leaves** odd-
pinnate, with fewer leaflets than others of
family, (usually 7, 9 or 11); leaflets rounded-
oval, blunt, somewhat pubescent underneath.

The root is considered edible.

Moist slopes, heath, arctic and alpine
tundra.

AK | YT

131

ANDY FYON

JULIA CARR

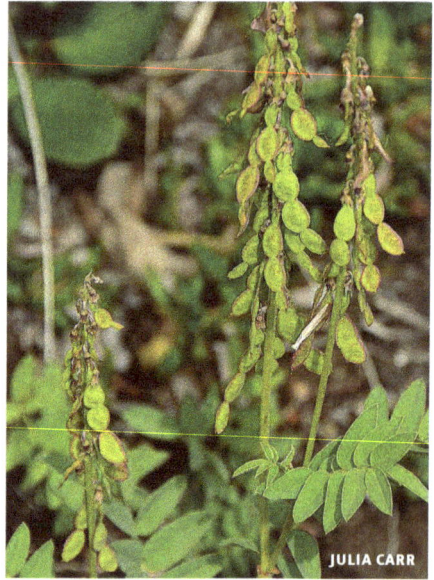

Hedysarum americanum

ALPINE SWEET-VETCH, ESKIMO POTATO

SYNONYM *Hedysarum alpinum*
Perennial herb from a branched, woody base and thick taproot. **Flowers** pea-like, rose-magenta, turning purplish as they fade, a dozen or more on one side of a spike-like stem; calyx triangular; followed by flat seed pods. **Stems** erect (to 2 feet), often much branched and stout, rise from a tuber-like root; later in season the plant stems are more lax. **Leaves** pinnate (up to 20 leaflets); leaflets with rounded base, oblong, pointed, rather thin and conspicuously veined.

The enlarged root is edible, either raw or cooked. However, Chris McCandless (*Into the Wild*) prior to his death in the Alaskan wilderness, recorded in his diary his illness brought on by eating the seeds of a *Hedysarum*.

Open woods, gravelly slopes, tundra, roadsides.

AK **YT**

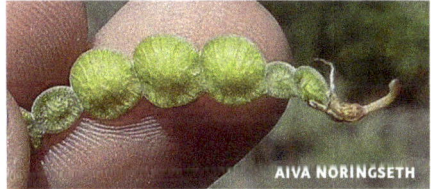

Hedysarum boreale

BOREAL SWEET-VETCH

SYNONYM *Hedysarum mackenzii*
Perennial herb from a branched, woody base and thick taproot. **Flowers** pea-like, rose to purple, in a showy long panicle or spike, fragrant; calyx long, linear; followed by a flat seed pod. **Stems** erect, to 1½ feet, branching, hairy. Flower stems rise from leaf axils. **Leaves** pinnate (with up to 17 leaflets), long-oval, round-ended, rather thick leaflets, grayish on underside.

In contrast to *Hedysarum americanum,* this is not an edible plant; the root is reportedly poisonous. Gravelly or sandy soil, rocky slopes, river bars, roadsides.

AK YT

Lathyrus japonicus

BEACH PEA

SYNONYM *Lathyrus maritimus*
Perennial herb from a rhizome. **Flowers** pea-like, purple-magenta, 3–8 in a loose panicle which rises from a leaf axil. **Stems** creeping, long, slender, much-branched. **Leaves** pinnate, with 3–6 pairs of broad, oval, round-ended leaflets, somewhat thick, with a terminal, sometimes branched, tendril.

Pods edible, both raw and cooked.
Beaches, bases of cliffs, coastal areas.

AK YT

STEPHANIE ZELENESKY

DARYL COULSON

NOAHDORE

Lathyrus palustris

MARSH PEA

Perennial herb from a slender rhizome.
Flowers pea-like, royal purple, in groups of
3–8. **Stems** creeping (to 2 feet), slender.
Leaves pinnate, with 2–4 pairs of lance-
shaped, pointed, rather stiff, coarse leaflets,
with a terminal tendril.

Moist woods, wet meadows, tidal flats,
beaches.

AK

135 ■

JOHANN WAGNER

DREW BRAYSHAW

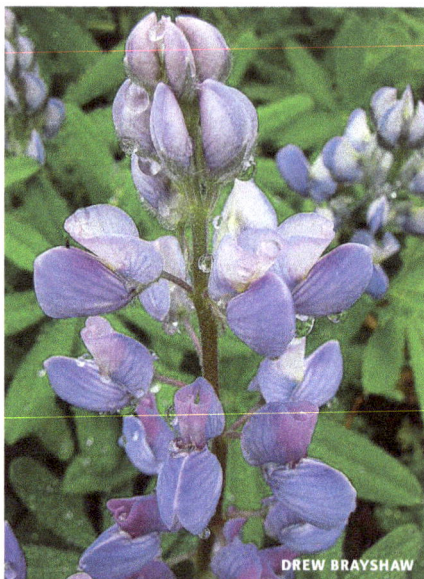

Lupinus arcticus

ARCTIC LUPINE

Perennial herb from a branched, woody base. **Flowers** pea-like, purple (often white-tipped), fragrant, in a thick, pointed, spike-like cluster on a single stem. **Stems** erect (to 15 inches), stout, usually grows in clumps. **Leaves** palmately compound, attractive, with 5–10 narrow, pointed leaflets; basal leaves on long petioles.

One of Alaska's beautiful flowers, it grows at both high and low elevations and in all types of soil.

Poisonous, especially the seeds.

Note that Yukon and Nootka lupines have small hairs on the upper surface of their leaves, while leaves of this species are without hairs.

Arctic and alpine tundra, heath, woods, roadsides; more widespread than the other two lupines described here.

AK YT

AVERY BARTELS

MITCH GARDINER

AVERY BRENDANN QUERY

Lupinus kuschei

YUKON LUPINE

Perennial herb from a woody base; entire plant (except the corollas) densely silvery silky-hairy. **Flowers** many in a dense, stalked, terminal raceme of whorled pea-like flowers; corolla blue to bluish purple, the banner with a yellow central patch. **Stems** decumbent to erect (to about 15 inches), few to several, tufted. **Leaves** palmately compound, with 5–9 leaflets.

This lupine is known only from south-western Yukon Territory, adjacent northern British Columbia, and east-central Alaska.

Sand dunes, open sandy woods, road-sides.

AK YT

137 ■

OKSANA

MIALEVINE

Lupinus nootkatensis

NOOTKA LUPINE

Perennial herb from a stout, woody base. **Flowers** pea-like, purple (often partially white), in dense, pointed spike. **Stems** erect (to well over 2 feet), branched, clustered, stout (a taller, stouter plant than *Lupinus arcticus*). **Leaves** palmately compound, attractive, short-petioled and mostly basal; leaflets long-oval, blunt tipped.

The casual observer would probably see no difference between these two lupines, but this species is larger, its leaves are more blunt, and it has more flowering stems. In the Yukon, found only in the southwest mountains; more widely distributed in southern half of Alaska.

Poisonous, especially the seeds.

Mountain slopes, meadows, gravel bars.

AK YT

TOBIAS GRATZER

KATERINA KASHIRINA

Melilotus alba, Melilotus officinalis

WHITE SWEET-CLOVER, YELLOW SWEET-CLOVER

Annual or biennial herb from a taproot. These are the wild sweet-clovers. Both species found in Alaska are introduced plants, and both are very well-established along roads. **Flowers** white or yellow, tiny, in slender, spike-like racemes; fragrant. **Stems** erect, up to 5 feet, much-branched. *Melilotus alba* has the stouter stem. **Leaves** of three-toothed leaflets, alternate, and rather inconspicuous; those of *Melilotus officinalis* are broader.

Sometimes treated as a single species, *Melilotus officinalis*.

Roadsides, waste places.

AK YT

139 ■

DRONSSE

ANDY LYON

THOMPSON HYGGEN

Oxytropis bryophila

YUKON LOCOWEED

SYNONYM *Oxytropis nigrescens*

Perennial herb from a taproot. **Flowers** pea-like, purple, usually solitary (or a pair), terminal on stem. **Stems** short, matted (1½–3 inches), slender, rising directly from root. **Leaves** odd-pinnate, with about 9 tiny, gray-green, lanceolate, pointed leaflets; the petioles of the leaves also rise directly from the root.

Members of this genus should not be eaten, and can cause livestock to act erratically, hence the common name.

Rocky alpine slopes, tundra.

AK YT

■ 140

SARAH GREGG

MICHAEL G. SHEPARD

SARAH GREGG

Oxytropis campestris

FIELD LOCOWEED

Perennial, tufted, hairy herb from a taproot. **Flowers** pea-like, yellowish or cream-colored, 5–30 in a rather fat, rounded head. **Stems** erect (6-10 inches), stout; the flower stem rises from root. **Leaves** odd-pinnate (with 13–15 leaflets), small, lanceolate, pointed, widely spaced, grayish green, on petioles which rise from the root.

Woods, heath, gravel bars, rock outcrops, from sea-level to alpine.

AK YT

141 ■

MATTHIAS BUCK

COLOCRITTERS

Oxytropis deflexa

PENDANT-POD LOCOWEED

Perennial herb from a taproot. **Flowers** pea-like, dingy yellowish white, many in an open, loose, somewhat oblong head. **Stems** erect (about 8–9 inches), a small, tufted plant, silvery gray. **Leaves** pinnate (with 23–45 leaflets), silvery, silky gray, lanceolate, rounded at base, pointed at tip.

Leaves and stems erect and rigid when plant is young, becoming more lax as plant matures.

Woods, thickets, heath, usually on sandy or gravelly soils.

AK YT

CALLUM MCKENZIE

JOHN D REYNOLDS

AUSTIN SAUNDERS

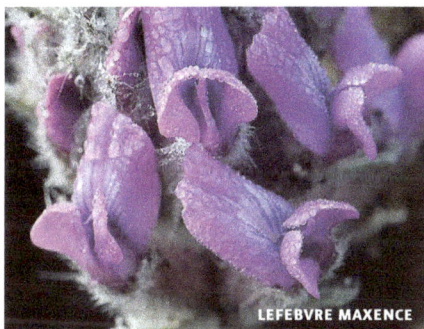
LEFEBVRE MAXENCE

Oxytropis splendens

SHOWY LOCOWEED

Perennial herb from a strong taproot and base covered with persistent stipules. **Flowers** pea-like, reddish-purple, many in a spike-like raceme, elongating in age. **Stems** tufted (to about 12 inches), densely silky-hairy. **Leaves** pinnately compound (with 32–70 leaflets), soft-hairy.

Open woods, riverbanks, clearings.

AK YT

143 ▪

ALSIKE CLOVER   KEIR MORSE

RED CLOVER   KEIR MORSE

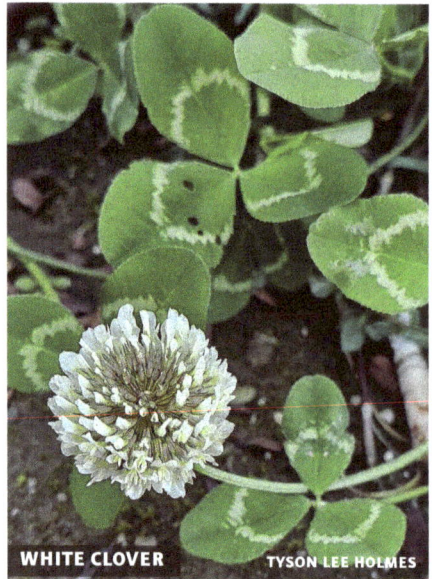

WHITE CLOVER   TYSON LEE HOLMES

Trifolium

CLOVER

Three of the most common clovers are described below; all are introductions from Europe and found on roadsides and in towns of Alaska and the Yukon. **Flowers** are small and pea-like, clustered into a tight head; **leaves** are 3-parted.

UPPER LEFT. **Alsike Clover** (*Trifolium hybridum*), flowers white and pink.

UPPER RIGHT. **Red Clover** (*Trifolium pratense*), flowers red and pink, larger than in Alsike or White Clover.

RIGHT. **White Clover** (*Trifolium repens*), flowers white.

AK YT

AVERY ALLERT

YURIPANOV

SNSERGEEVNA

Vicia cracca

TUFTED VETCH

Introduced perennial herb. **Flowers** pea-like, deep-purple, in a long, dense, one-sided, axillary raceme. **Stems** climbing or trailing (often 6 feet), slender. **Leaves** pinnate, with a terminal tendril; leaflets 4–12 pairs.

Roadsides, disturbed places.

AK YT

145 ■

JEAN-DOMINIQUE LEBRETON

BEN SCHMIDT

Gentiana glauca

PALE GENTIAN

Perennial herb from a slender rhizome. **Flowers** deep blue-green, shining, closed, about one inch long; two or three flowers upright at top of stem. **Stems** erect (2–3 inches), stout. **Leaves** ovate, small, rounded, spatulate, shiny, a few pairs on stem but mostly in a basal rosette.

The flowers are a most unusual color. Subalpine and alpine meadows, tundra.

AK YT

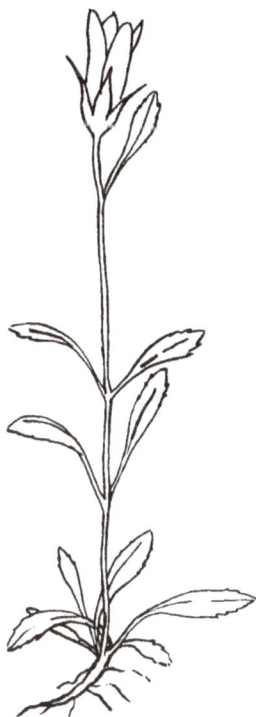

Gentiana prostrata

PYGMY GENTIAN

Annual or biennial herb from a slender tap-root. **Flowers** purple, bell-shaped, 4-lobed, slender, upturned; solitary at stem end; opening only on bright, sunny days. **Stems** prostrate to arched (about 4 inches), un-branched, leafy. **Leaves** small, slender, lin-ear, in pairs, slightly toothed toward tip.

Arctic and alpine tundra, heath, moist meadows.

AK YT

147

VLADIMIR BRYUKHOV

STANLEY DAVIS

CORY CHIAPPONE

Gentianella amarella

AUTUMN GENTIAN

SYNONYM *Gentiana amarella*
Annual or biennial herb from a taproot.
Flowers purple, bell-like, upturned; the terminal blossom large, those from nodes on short peduncles. **Stems** erect (to 8 inches), slender, delicate. **Leaves** long-oval, pointed, delicate, in sessile pairs at nodes of stem.

Open woods, moist meadows, streambanks.

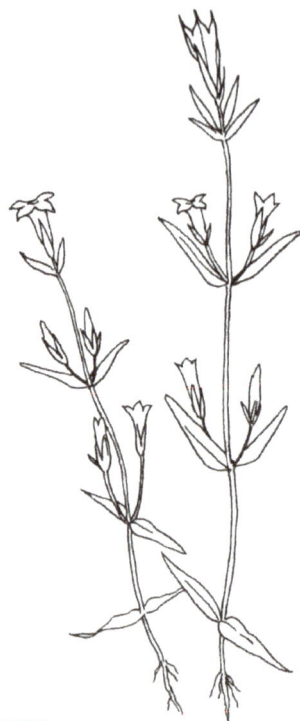

AK YT

■ 148

MEGGO EDGAR

SCOTT NIELSEN

Gentianella propinqua

FOUR-PART DWARF-GENTIAN

SYNONYM *Gentiana propinqua*
Annual herb from a taproot. **Flowers** purple, slender bell-shaped, with pointed lobes, upturned; small, except the terminal one; on very long pedicels, several rise from each node. **Stems** erect (to 15 inches), very slender, branched, often brownish-purple. **Leaves** lanceolate, pointed, sessile in pairs on stem, with a small group of larger, basal leaves.

The tallest of our gentians.

Arctic and alpine tundra, woods, mountain slopes.

AK YT

149 ■

MARIA AND WOLFGANG ROSENWIRTH

ABBY HYDE

EVA ULLSTRÖM

Swertia perennis

FELWORT, STAR-GENTIAN

Perennial herb from a short, thick rhizome. **Flowers** royal purple, shaped like a five-pointed star, on 2-inch individual stems from leaf axils. **Stems** erect (to 2 feet), coarse, stiff-appearing. **Leaves** oblanceolate, long, spatulate, in pairs; the stem leaves small, sessile, sparse; lower leaves long and on long petioles.

Moist woods, meadows, streambanks, often shaded by other tall plants.

AK YT

JEREMY ATHERTON

TOM ARMSTRONG

JASPER SHIDE

Geranium bicknellii

NORTHERN CRANE'S-BILL

Annual or biennial herb from a taproot.
Flowers purple to rose-lavender, usually in
pairs at stem end; petals 5, small; sepals
hairy. **Stems** erect (6–10 inches), branched.
Leaves pentagonal in outline with deeply
cut and toothed segments; small leaves
present among the blossoms, otherwise all
are basal.

Roadsides, open woods; weedy.

AK **YT**

PAVEL SMIRNOV

SANTIAGO MARTÍN-BRAVO

DARRIN GOBBLE

Geranium erianthum

WOOLLY CRANE'S-BILL

Perennial herb from a thick base or rhizome. **Flowers** in varying shades of purple-blue, on short peduncles, in small groups at stem ends; petals 5, red-veined, good-sized; after petals fall the red stamens persist; sepals silky hairy. **Stems** erect (to 18 inches), stout, leafy, branched, silky hairy. **Leaves** palmately lobed, with many toothed divisions, silky on underside.

An attractive and widely distributed plant which begins to flower just as *Mertensia paniculata* begins to fade.

Woods, meadows, alpine slopes.

AK YT

■ 152

EMMA READER-LEE

JOHN BREW

KIERAN HANRAHAN

LEE CAIN

Ribes bracteosum

STINK CURRANT

Deciduous shrub. **Flowers** greenish white, simple, small, many on a long, upright raceme; followed by blue-black berries with a whitish bloom. **Stems** erect (to several feet), a vigorous, branched, woody shrub; bark brownish, with round, yellow, crystal-like glands. **Leaves** large, palmate, with 5–7 large lobes with toothed edges, thin, with resinous spots on underside.

Plants not prickly, with a pungent odor.

Woods, thickets, streambanks; coastal regions of southern Alaska.

AK

ALAINA KRAKOWIAK

J S REIFF

LAURA J. COSTELLO

Ribes glandulosum

SKUNK CURRANT

Deciduous shrub. **Flowers** whitish to red, with 7–10 in a slender raceme; followed by large, red, bristly fruit. **Stems** somewhat decumbent, long, bristly, woody. **Leaves** palmate, 5–7 lobed, sharply toothed, in outline like a maple.

Low-elevation woods, rocky slopes.

AK YT

NOAH HOW

TOM SCAVO

MARK POLLOCK

Ribes lacustre

SWAMP GOOSEBERRY

Deciduous shrub. **Flowers** pinkish, in racemes; followed by a shiny, black, prickly fruit. **Stems** erect (3–6 feet), branched, bristly, a vigorous woody plant. **Leaves** 5–7 lobed, pentagonal in general outline, toothed, bristly.

Moist woods, streambanks, thickets.

AK YT

155 ■

JENNY KIRKPATRICK

KATHERINE BAIRD

KATHERINE BAIRD

Ribes laxiflorum

TRAILING BLACK CURRANT

Deciduous shrub. **Flowers** pinkish-white, small, in 6–12-flowered racemes, these often erect; fruit black, egg-shaped, with stalked bristly glands, and with an unpleasant odor. **Stems** decumbent, trailing, long, woody. **Leaves** with five deeply cut toothed lobes, smooth, on long petioles.

Moist woods, thickets.

AK YT

JACK BINDERNAGEL

LAURALASKA66

JAY BRASHER

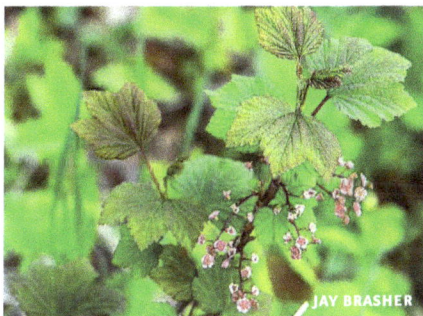

Ribes triste

SWAMP RED CURRANT

Deciduous shrub. **Flowers** brick red; petals 4–5, small; many flowers on a short green stem; blooms very early, followed by a smooth, red, very tart berry, ripening in July, and similar to our cultivated currant. **Stems** straggly (18 inches to 4 feet), not prickly, with reddish-brown, woody bark. **Leaves** kidney-shaped, 3–5-lobed, toothed, small, smooth above and hairy underneath.

A much-prized edible fruit.

Moist, shaded woods, thickets.

AK YT

157 ■

ALEXANDRIA WENNINGER

OLEG KÖSTERIN

JASON GRANT

Iris setosa

BEACH-HEAD IRIS

Perennial herb. **Flowers** pale blue-lavender to deep purple, one on a stem. **Stems** erect (12–18 inches), fleshy, gray-green. **Leaves** long, slender, sword-like, gray-green, a few small ones on stem but leaves mostly basal.

Poisonous, causes vomiting if eaten.

Wet meadows, shores, tidal flats. Uncommon in the Yukon (southwestern Yukon only).

AK YT

■ 158

Dracocephalum parviflorum

AMERICAN DRAGONHEAD

Annual or biennial herb from a taproot.
Flowers in dense spikes; corolla blue or
purplish to pinkish, with two short lips, the
lower lip 3-lobed. **Stems** erect (to about 2
feet), 4-angled; minutely hairy with stiff
hairs. **Leaves** opposite, lanceolate, coarsely
toothed with the teeth often spine-tipped;
lower leaves smaller, broader, and soon deciduous.

Disturbed places, especially where
recently burned.

AK YT

ALEXIS TINKER-TSAVALAS

MICHAEL NEWLON

TOM SCAVO

Prunella vulgaris

COMMON SELFHEAL

Perennial herb. **Flowers** deep purple, very small, among green bracts in a short, dense, solitary, terminal spike. **Stems** erect (4 inches or more), rather stout. **Leaves** lance-olate, shallowly toothed, narrow into a peti-ole at the base; an opposite pair at base of flower head, others basal.

Moist woods, meadows, talus slopes.

AK YT

■ 160

LEEANN LATREMOUILLE

BOUKE TEN CATE

MATT BOWSER

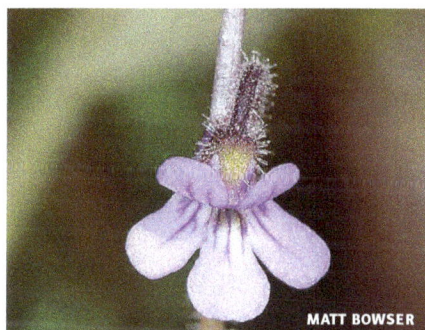

Pinguicula villosa

HAIRY BUTTERWORT

Insect-eating perennial herb from a fibrous root. **Flowers** purplish, tiny, spurred, solitary at end of stem. **Stems** erect (about 3 inches), slender, very finely hairy. **Leaves** broad, thick, small, sticky, all basal in a tiny rosette.

A small, attractive plant, easily overlooked.

Sphagnum moss bogs.

AK YT

161 ■

CRICKET RASPET

J STRAKA

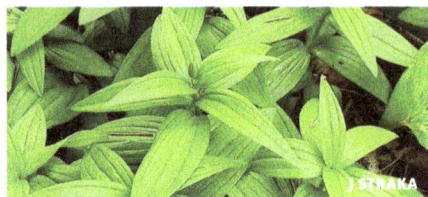

Fritillaria camschatcensis

CHOCOLATE LILY, RICE-ROOT

Perennial herb. **Flowers** dark purplish-brown, nodding, often yellowish green on back near stem, 1–4 on a stalk. **Stems** erect (1–2 feet), stout, rising from a scaly bulb which is made up of tiny bulblets. **Leaves** lanceolate, long, narrow, pointed, often in a whorl around the stem.

The rice-like bulblets and young seeds are edible, either raw or cooked. The flowers have an unpleasant scent leading to another common name of 'Skunk Lily.'

Moist woods and meadows, at both low and high elevations; plants often in deep grass.

AK YT

NOLAN EXE

THIERRY ARBAULT

MATT MUIR

Gagea serotina

ALP-LILY

SYNONYM *Lloydia serotina*
Perennial herb. **Flowers** white, bell-shaped, usually solitary, nodding; petals 3, each with a brown stripe. **Stems** erect (4–5 inches), slender, from a bulb and creeping rootstock. **Leaves** fine and grass-like, smaller leaves alternate on stem but chiefly basal.

Distinctive, and not easily confused with any other small plant of the region.

Rock ledges, dry alpine and arctic tundra.

AK YT

163 ■

CALEB CATTO

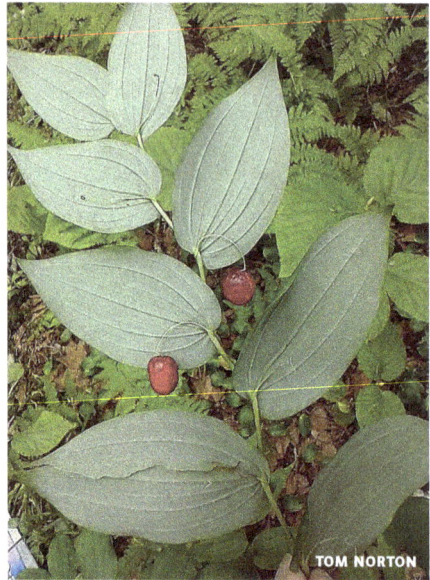
TOM NORTON

Streptopus amplexifolius

CLASPING TWISTED-STALK, CUCUMBER ROOT

Perennial herb from a short, thick rhizome. **Flowers** creamy-white, bell-shaped, drooping, single on short pedicels attached to the underside of the leaf at its base; tepals (the similar petals and sepals) 6; followed by a long, oval, red berry. **Stems** graceful (to about 3 feet), often branched, with fine blackish hairs on lower portion. **Leaves** broadly lanceolate, large, pointed, thin, with noticeable parallel veins, alternate, clasping the stem.

Springtime shoots can be eaten raw (having a taste similar to cucumber), or cooked; the berries are used in jellies.

Moist meadows, woods.

AK YT

■ 164

NORTHCUT

JACK BINDERNAGEL

ZACH E PLANTS

Linum lewisii

WILD BLUE FLAX

Glabrous and somewhat glaucous perennial herb, from a woody crown. **Flowers** in a terminal raceme, on slender pedicels about as long as the flowers; petals 5, blue; stamens 5; styles 5, much longer than the stamens. **Stems** to 2 feet tall. **Leaves** alternate, linear, about 1 inch long.

Fibers of *Linum* used to make linen and the seeds for linseed oil.

Dry, sandy soils at low-elevations.

AK | YT

165

Anticlea elegans

MOUNTAIN DEATHCAMAS

SYNONYM *Zigadenus elegans*
Perennial herb. **Flowers** yellow-green, small, with a darker spot on each of the 3 petals; several in a loose, terminal raceme. **Stems** erect (8–12 inches), solitary, rather stout, with a few stem leaves, arising from a deep bulb. **Leaves** long, narrow, pointed, lily-like, gray-green and somewhat waxy, mostly basal.

Highly poisonous.

Meadows, dry slopes, open woods.

AK YT

AIVA NORINGSETH

TOM SCAVO

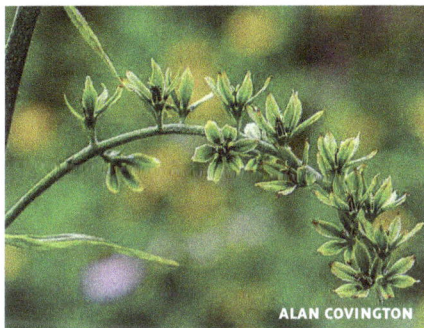

ALAN COVINGTON

Veratrum viride

GREEN FALSE HELLEBORE

Perennial herb. **Flowers** greenish yellow, on a very tall spike with drooping branches; petals 3, small; followed by flat, winged seeds. **Stems** erect (often 6 feet), stout and fleshy, from a stout rootstock. **Leaves** lanceolate, long, fleshy, strongly veined, fuzzy on underside; young leaves closely wrapped around the stem.

Highly poisonous.

Alpine meadows, heathlands.

AK YT

167 ■

CALEB CATTO

BRYN

CHRISTIAN BACK

Menyanthes trifoliata

BUCKBEAN, BOG BEAN

Perennial semi-aquatic herb from a thick rhizome. **Flowers** white (pinkish in bud), petals 5, fringed. **Stems** erect (to 12 inches), smooth, fleshy, hollow, rising above the water from a creeping rootstock. **Leaves** large, trifoliate, fleshy, shiny dark green; the lobes are broad, oval, pointed; on a long, stout petiole.

Distinctive as it flowers early and the plants are in standing water. In the past, a tea from the leaves or dried roots was used medicinally.

Shallow water of lakes, ponds, and bogs, often forming large colonies.

AK YT

SAMUELLE SIMARD-PROVENÇAL

SIMONE

BELVEDERE04

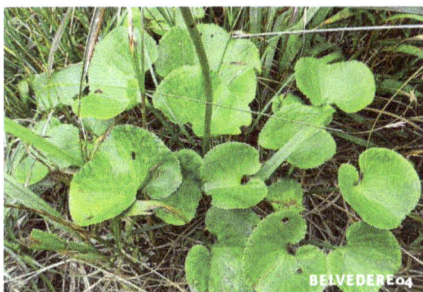

Nephrophyllidium crista-galli

DEER-CABBAGE

SYNONYM *Fauria crista-galli*

Perennial herb from a thick rhizome. **Flowers** pink and white, foul-smelling; petals 5, stamens exerted; flowers in terminal groups, some from leaf axils and intermixed with leafy bracts. **Stems** erect (8–12 inches), stout, hairy, leafy, rising from a thick rootstock. **Leaves** large, thick, rounded, evenly scalloped, glabrous, ridged, on long petioles.

Bogs, swamps, seeps; coastal southern and southeastern Alaska.

AK

169 ■

LAURALASKA66

ALEXANDRIA WENNINGER

ALASKA66

Claytonia sarmentosa

ALASKA SPRINGBEAUTY

Perennial herb. **Flowers** pinkish lavender, 2–3 terminal on stem; petals 5 each with purple vein, large relative to remainder of plant. **Stems** weak, about 3 inches, very slender, with stolons from base of stem. **Leaves** on stem somewhat oval, sessile, blunt; basal leaves ovate, spatulate, narrowing into a petiole.

The leaves are edible.

Wet alpine slopes and streambanks, often near the edge of melting snow.

AK YT

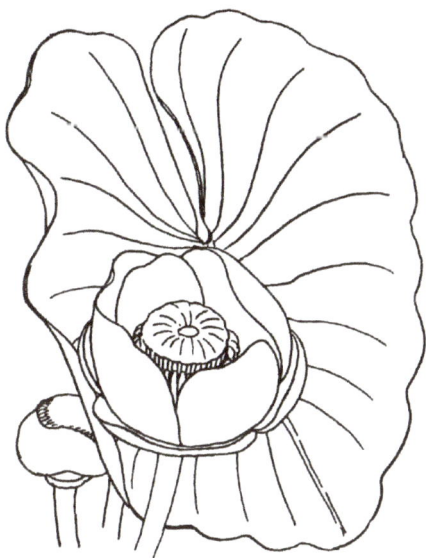

Nuphar polysepala

YELLOW POND-LILY

Perennial aquatic herb from a thick large rhizome. **Flowers** deep butter-yellow, solitary, wide (3 inches), cup-like, on a long stem; petals numerous, large, stiff, waxy, with disk center. **Stems** erect from a thick underwater horizontal rootstock. **Leaves** large, round to heart-shaped, deep-green, fleshy, floating, up to 1 foot wide.

Long-used as a food by native peoples, the thick rootstock was boiled and eaten, and the seeds used as a grain or popped like popcorn. Also a food for beaver, and the roots are especially favored by moose.

Ponds, slow-moving streams.

AK YT

171

OLEG KOSTERIN

OLEG KOSTERIN

OLEG KOSTERIN

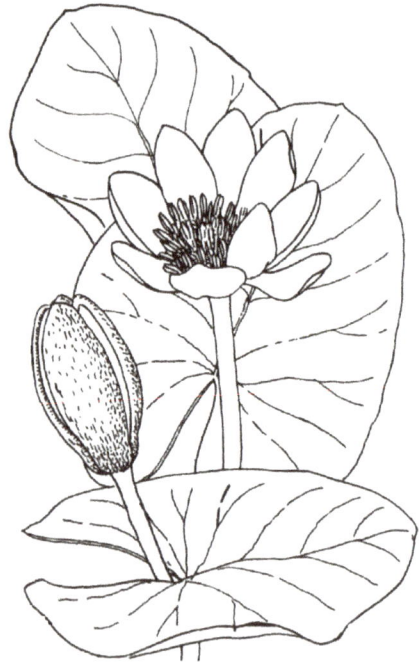

Nymphaea tetragona

WHITE WATER LILY

Perennial aquatic herb from a thick, upright rhizome. **Flowers** white with yellow centers; petals 6–10, showy, pointed. **Stems** fleshy, rising above the water from underwater roots. **Leaves** ovate, with open sinus, thick, dark-green, floating, on long stems.

Lakes, ponds, swamps.

AK **YT**

ELIAS

MARK POLLOCK

TIMOTHY MCNITT

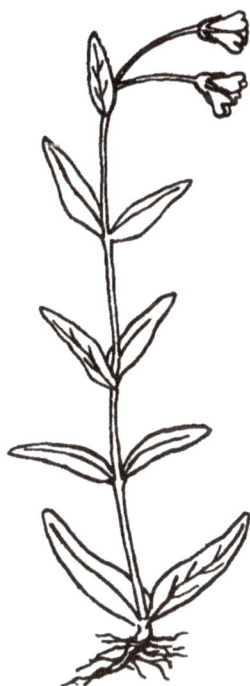

Epilobium anagallidifolium

PIMPERNEL WILLOWHERB

SYNONYM *Epilobium alpinum*

Perennial herb from a fibrous root, may form mats. **Flowers** deep pink with a darker vein, nodding, one or two from end of stem; petals 4, tiny, usually partly closed. **Stems** erect or arched, about 3–5 inches, slender, leafy. **Leaves** long oval, blunt, often brownish green, opposite on stem.

A delicate plant.

Moist or wet soils.

AK YT

173

CALEB CATTO

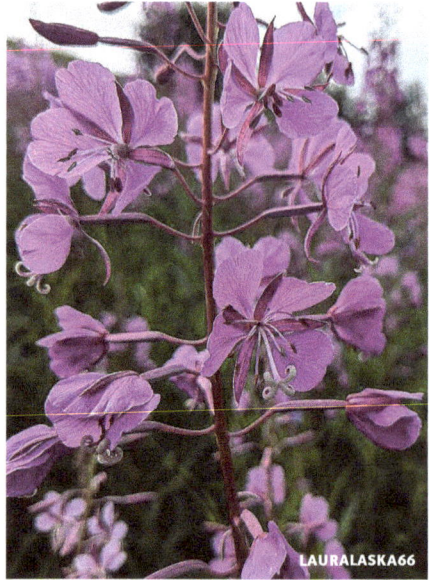

LAURALASKA66

Epilobium angustifolium

FIREWEED

SYNONYM *Chamaenerion angustifolium*
Perennial herb from widely spreading rhizome-like root. **Flowers** magenta or rose-purple (though pure white and pale pink specimens are occasionally found), on pedicels, many on a tall raceme; petals 4, sepals 4 of a darker shade. The seed case splits and releases silky, wind-carried seeds. **Stems** erect (to 3 feet or more), stout, smooth, red when plant is old. **Leaves** willow-like, long, narrow, pointed, alternate, smooth on upper side, many on stem; leaf veins turn deep red when plant is old.

A widely distributed, very striking plant; rapidly colonizing burned-over areas, and the official flower of the Yukon Territory. The new, red sprouts can be cooked and eaten as greens; a valuable honey plant.

Meadows, woods, tundra, recent burns, roadsides.

AK YT

PETER ACHUFF

AIVA NORINGSETH

Epilobium latifolium

DWARF FIREWEED

SYNONYM *Chamaenerion latifolium*
Perennial herb from a stout base, without rhizomes, often forming colonies. **Flowers** purple to rose, from upper leaf axils; petals 4 (much larger than those of Epilobium angustifolium). **Stems** sometimes not quite erect (6–12 inches), stout, often branched, leafy, gray-green and fuzzy. **Leaves** long-ovate, pointed, somewhat thick, light gray-green, fuzzy on both sides.

This is a very attractive and one of Alaska's most-loved wildflowers (gracing the cover of this book). The young sprouts are edible.

Streambanks, river bars, rocky slopes, roadsides.

AK YT

175 ■

VALERII GLAZUNOV

IKELMAN

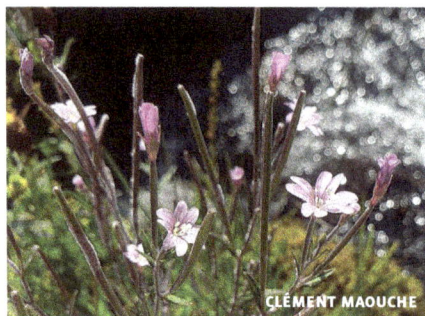

CLÉMENT MAOUCHE

Epilobium palustre

MARSH WILLOWHERB

Perennial herb from a slender rhizome, stolons threadlike. **Flowers** magenta, bell-like, small, one to many, terminal; petals 4. **Stems** erect or curved (8–18 inches), slender. **Leaves** mostly opposite, nearly linear to lanceolate, blunt-tipped.

Very much like *Epilobium anagallidifolium* except taller and with a narrower leaf.

Streambanks, roadside ditches, generally where wet.

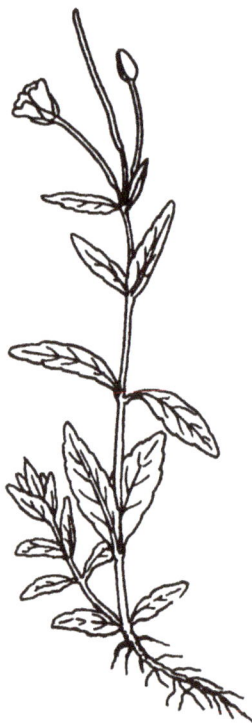

AK YT

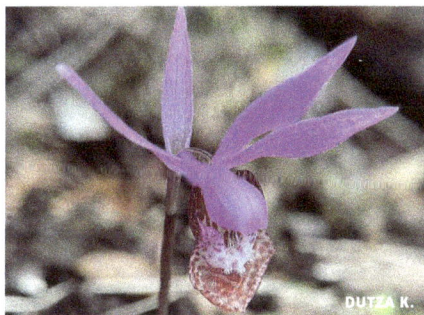

Calypso bulbosa

CALYPSO, FAIRY-SLIPPER ORCHID

Perennial herb from fleshy corm. **Flowers** purplish-pink, a solitary terminal bloom; upper petals narrow, lower petal sac-like, with yellow-brown spots. **Stems** erect (3–6 inches), slender, sheathed near base. **Leaf** single, broad, ovate, basal.

Very showy, one of the earliest wildflowers of the Matanuska Valley (mid- to late-May).

Dry to moist mossy woods.

AK YT

MILAN CHYTRÝ

ELIAS

DAVID SANDLER

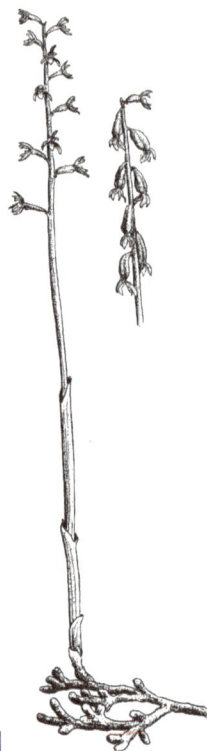

Corallorhiza trifida

YELLOW CORALROOT

Perennial, saprophytic herb from coral-like rhizomes. **Flowers** small, in a terminal raceme of 3-20; sepals and lateral petals similar, greenish yellow; lip broadly ovate, notched at tip, with a pair of small lobes at base, whitish and often spotted with purple. **Stems** yellowish brown, smooth, to about 10 inches tall. **Leaves** few, reduced to sheathing bracts. **Capsules** drooping.

Woods, thickets, especially on calcium-rich soils.

AK YT

■ 178

LAURALASKA66

ELENA KIZILOVA

NURKHAYDAROVA TATIANA

Cypripedium guttatum

SPOTTED LADY'S-SLIPPER

Perennial herb from rhizomes, with coarse fibrous roots. **Flowers** solitary, drooping; with upper petals white edged with rose, lower petals a sac, mottled with deep pinkish purple. **Stems** erect (6–8 inches), with one small leaf behind the blossom. **Leaves** broad, lanceolate, pointed, many-veined, with one pair of basal leaves from the horizontal rootstock.

Meadows, woods, heathlands.

AK YT

179 ■

CALEB CATTO

JACK BINDERNAGEL

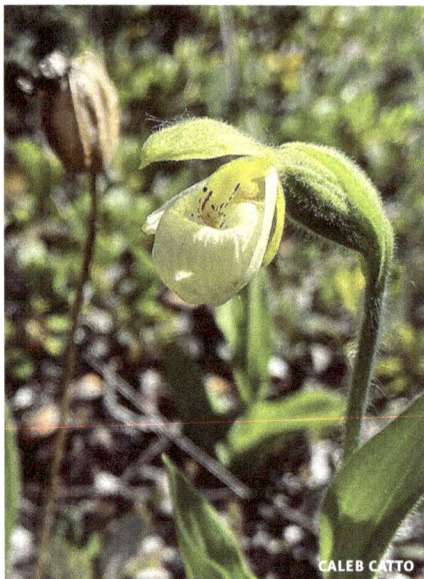

CALEB CATTO

Cypripedium passerinum

SPARROW-EGG LADY'S-SLIPPER

Perennial herb from slender rhizomes, with coarse fibrous roots. **Flowers** 1–3 at end of stems; lateral petals white; lip pouch-like, white, faintly purple-spotted on inside. **Stems** to about 12 inches tall, with long, soft hairs. **Stem leaves** 3–5, elliptic, sticky-hairy, ribbed, sheathing stem at their base.

In bloom in late-June and July.

Sphagnum bogs, mossy woods, shores, wet rocky slopes.

AK YT

CHLOE & TREVOR VAN LOON

JACK BINDERNAGEL

MEGAN BLACKMORE

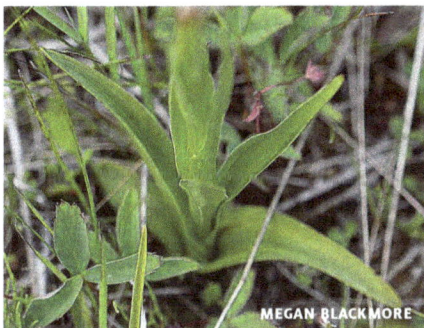

Platanthera dilatata

WHITE BOG-ORCHID, BOG-CANDLE

SYNONYM *Habenaria dilatata*
Perennial herb with a few fibrous roots.
Flowers white, small, fragrant, spurred,
borne loosely on a terminal spike; the base
of the lip is dilated. **Stems** erect (to 1 foot),
solitary, fleshy. **Stem leaves** fleshy, narrow,
pointed; lower leaves lanceolate and blunt.

Coastal areas; inland in muskegs, bogs,
on shores; wet, grassy meadows.

AK YT

181 ■

MARTINE LAPOINTE

IDA B D JACOBSEN

MARTINE LAPOINTE

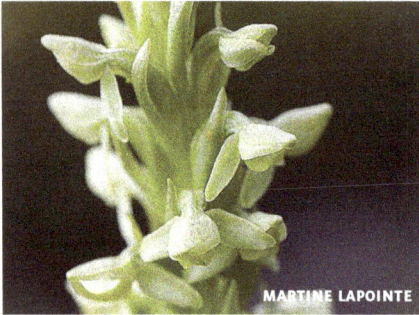

Platanthera hyperborea

NORTHERN GREEN ORCHID

SYNONYM *Habenaria hyperborea*
Perennial herb. **Flowers** greenish yellow, in a rather dense, slender spike; spur curved, thickened; lip narrow linear-lanceolate. **Stems** erect (6–16 inches), solitary, fleshy. **Stem leaves** small, lanceolate; lower stem leaves broad, long oval, blunt, smooth in texture.

  Bogs, wet meadows, streambanks, shores.

AK YT

SHAAN AROESTE

CALEB CATTO

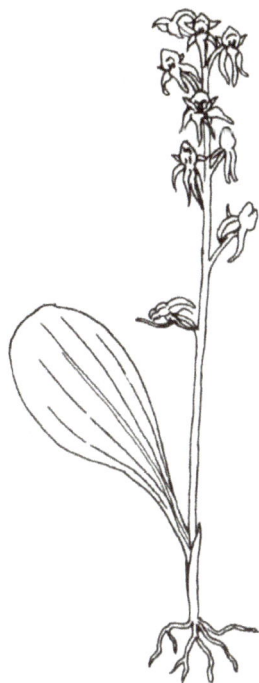

AK YT

Platanthera obtusata

BLUNT-LEAF ORCHID, SMALL NORTHERN BOG-ORCHID

SYNONYM *Habenaria obtusata*
Perennial herb, from a few fleshy-tuberous roots. **Flowers** greenish yellow, slender; spur slightly curved; lip narrow; flowers somewhat larger than in *Platanthera hyperborea,* but less numerous and in a looser inflorescence. **Stems** erect (to 8 inches), slender, glabrous, leafless. **Leaf** single at base of stem, wide, obovate, blunt, spatulate.

Flowering somewhat later than other species of *Platanthera.*

Mossy woods, muskegs, thickets, streamsides.

183 ■

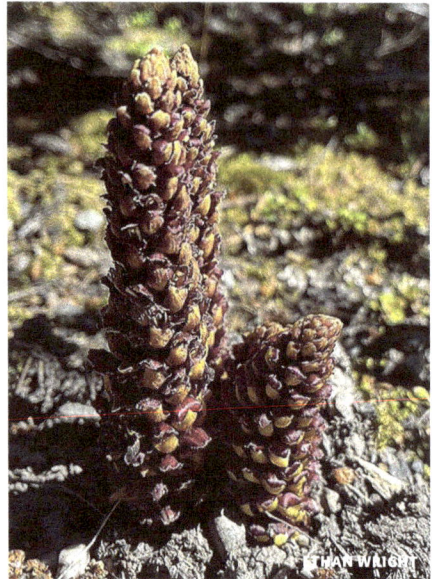

Boschniakia rossica

NORTHERN GROUNDCONE

Parasitic herb from a coarse fleshy root and thickened base. **Flowers** many, in a dense spike, each flower subtended by a bract; corollas rusty-red. **Stems** single or clustered (4–5 inches tall), stout, brownish, with glandular hairs. **Stem leaves** scale-like, overlapping like the bracts on a conifer cone; basal leaves absent.

Thickets, woods, heath, tundra, most commonly found among alders (*Alnus*), where parasitic on the roots.

AK YT

NPS, JACOB W. FRANK

KATHERINE BAIRD

LAURA MASKELL

NPS, JACOB W. FRANK

Castilleja elegans

ELEGANT INDIAN-PAINTBRUSH

Tufted perennial herb, from a short branching taproot, partly parasitic on roots of grasslike plants. **Flowers** (bracts) overlapping, purplish, or some with yellowish tips, in a terminal head; the actual flowers are very small and hidden by the colorful bracts. **Stems** several, erect (about 10 inches), purplish. **Leaves** pubescent, linear, entire or often with a pair of lateral lobes near tip.

Rocky alpine slopes and ridges, talus slopes, tundra, rocky or sandy lakeshores.

AK | YT

185 ◼

Castilleja pallida

PALE YELLOW INDIAN-PAINTBRUSH

Perennial herb, partly parasitic on roots of grasslike plants. **Flowers** pale-yellow, of overlapping bracts (these appearing like actual flowers) to form a large, dense, terminal head. **Stems** erect (to about 12 inches), sometimes branched, from an underground stem. **Leaves** lanceolate, rather narrow, long, pointed, sessile.

High-elevation meadows, woods, thickets.

AK YT

SUE CARNAHAN

ERIC LAMB

Pedicularis capitata

CAPITATE LOUSEWORT

Perennial herb from a slender rhizome. **Flowers** light creamy-yellow, large, beakless, 2–6 in a terminal cluster. **Stems** erect (about 5 inches), solitary, usually with 1–2 stem leaves. **Leaves** pinnate, deeply cut into about 9 leaflets, margins unevenly toothed, on a long petiole, a few from the rootstock.

Rocky alpine slopes, moist or dry tundra.

AK YT

187 ■

USFWS, ANCHORAGE OFFICE

ALEXEY SELEZNEV

Pedicularis labradorica

LABRADOR LOUSEWORT

Annual, biennial or short-lived perennial herb from a weak taproot. **Flowers** yellow (pinkish at some seasons), small, almost beakless, in an open cluster of 8–12, with a few in upper leaf axils. **Stems** erect (to 18 inches), much-branched (especially later in season), somewhat fuzzy, a few alternate leaves on stem. **Leaves** long, slender, pinnate, much-cut, fern-like, on short petioles.

Dry, gravelly alpine slopes; tundra, woods.

AK YT

■ 188

NIGEL VOADEN

TED CHEESEMAN

MATT MUIR

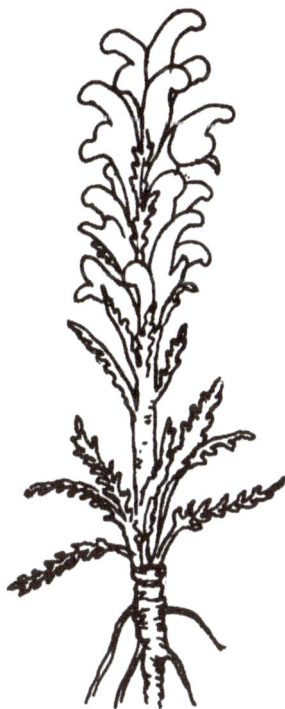

Pedicularis lanata

WOOLLY LOUSEWORT

Perennial herb from a thick yellow taproot.
Flowers pink, small to medium, many in a
dense, oblong, terminal spike with many
leafy woolly bracts. **Stems** erect (6 inches),
thick, short, gray-woolly, usually one from
a root. **Leaves** pinnate, long, slender, on
petioles, many on stem below flower head.

The thick, starchy taproot is edible.
Tundra, heathlands.

AK YT

189 ■

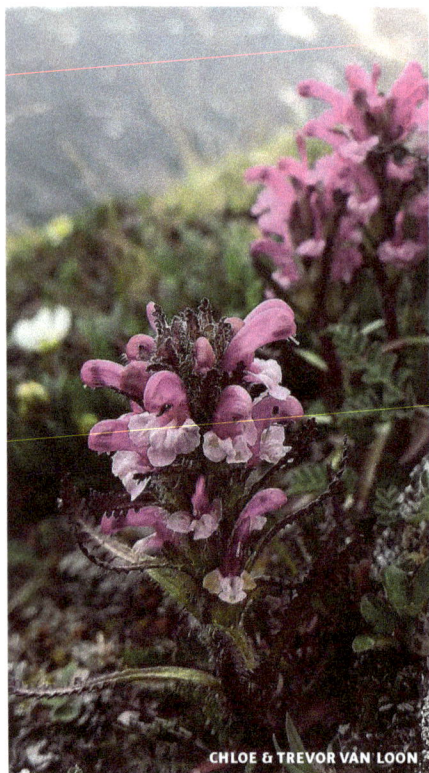

CHLOE & TREVOR VAN LOON

CHLOE & TREVOR VAN LOON

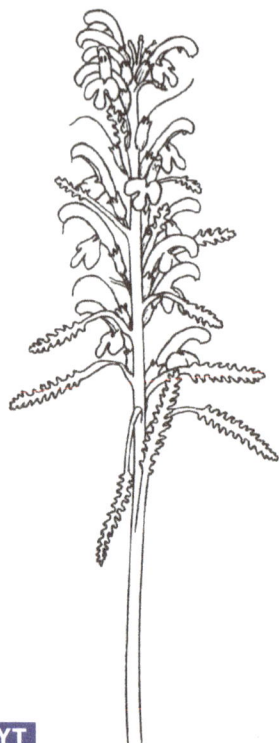

Pedicularis langsdorfii

LANGSDORF'S LOUSEWORT

Perennial herb from a thick yellow taproot. **Flowers** pink to purple, good-sized, curved but beakless, in a dense, terminal head with bracts. **Stems** erect (4–6 inches early, taller later in season); with several stout, leafy stems from one root. **Leaves** pinnate, long and narrow, each segment toothed; the leaves are the most noticeable characteristic of the plant.

Mountain slopes, tundra, heathlands.

AK YT

OLEG KOSTERIN

LEAH

CHRISTIAN BERG

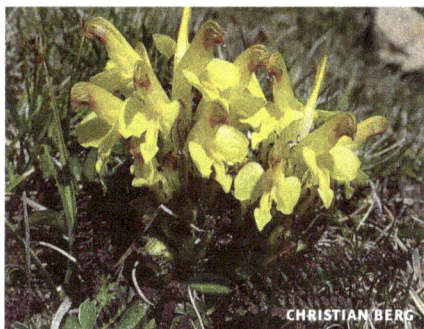

Pedicularis oederi

OEDER'S LOUSEWORT

Perennial herb from thickened roots. **Flowers** yellow, often with purple tips, very large, beaked; a few in large, terminal flower head with leafy bracts. **Stems** erect (about 6 inches), stout, with a few small stem leaves. **Leaves** long, pinnate, with segments toothed, on petioles, mostly in an attractive basal cluster.

Meadows, rocky slopes, tundra.

AK YT

191 ■

DUSTIN SNIDER

OWEN STRICKLAND

AIVA NORINGSETH

Pedicularis parviflora

SMALL-FLOWER LOUSEWORT

Annual or biennial herb from a weak tap-root. **Flowers** pinkish-purple, small, in leaf axils; a few in a very small flower head, giving an impression of more leaves than flowers. **Stems** erect (to about 10 inches), branched, leafy. **Leaves** large, very long, deeply dissected (as many as 14 pairs of leaflets), a few leaves on stem but more from the root.

Swamps, muskegs, wet meadows.

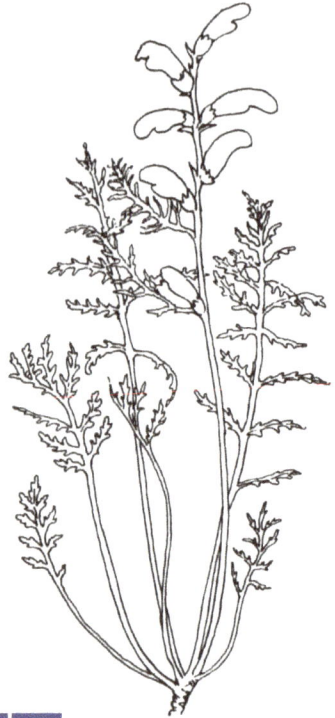

AK YT

VALERIJ GLAZUNOV

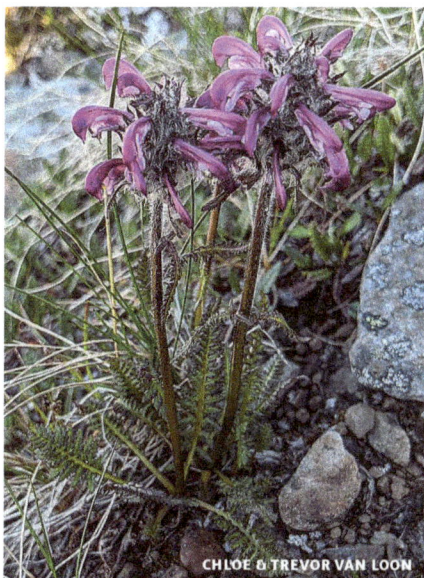

CHLOE & TREVOR VAN LOON

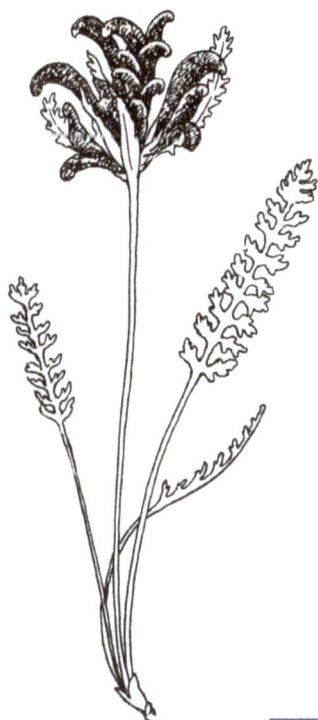

ERIC LAMB

Pedicularis sudetica

SUDETIC LOUSEWORT

Perennial herb from a stout rhizome. **Flowers** purplish, large, 6–8 in a broad, terminal spike. **Stems** erect (6 inches), solitary, stout, with several alternate leaves; later in season the stems elongate. **Leaves** pinnate, deeply cut (about 11 pairs of leaflets), on long petioles, a very attractive leaf.

Tundra, heathlands, sandy places.

AK | YT

193 ■

Pedicularis verticillata

WHORLED LOUSEWORT

Perennial herb from a taproot. **Flowers** pinkish purple (light inside), small, in a loose, terminal head, with a few flowers in upper leaf axils. **Stems** erect (6–8 inches), hairy, usually solitary. **Leaves** deeply pinnate, small, fuzzy; these are the most noticeable feature of the plant as they are arranged in whorls around the stem.

Meadows, rocky slopes, tundra.

AK YT

ROSACEAE_ROBERTS

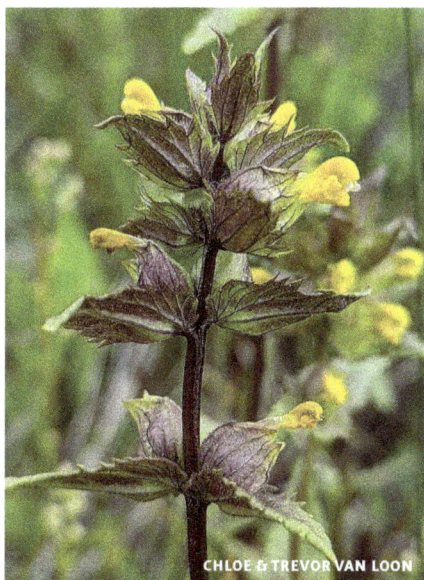

CHLOE & TREVOR VAN LOON

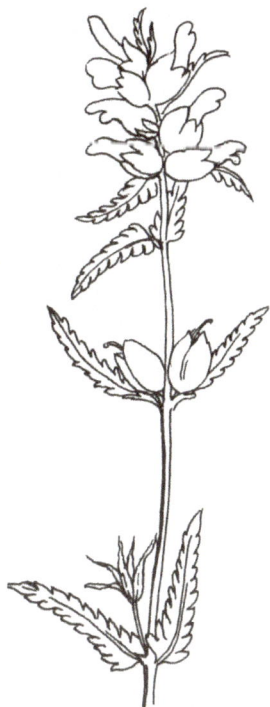

CALEB CATTO

Rhinanthus borealis

NORTHERN YELLOW-RATTLE

SYNONYM *Rhinanthus minor*

Annual herb. **Flowers** light-yellow, one petal a sac with lip, in leaf axils with leafy bracts, on a tall stem. **Stems** erect (12–18 inches), solitary, substantial. **Leaves** lance-shaped, long, narrow, pointed, with evenly serrate edges, in opposite pairs up the stem.

The common name refers to the ripened seeds which shake inside the enclosing calyx.

Fields, meadows, roadsides.

AK YT

195 ■

DAN MACNEAL

TOM ARMSTRONG

KEN-ICHI UEDA

Capnoides sempervirens

ROCK-HARLEQUIN

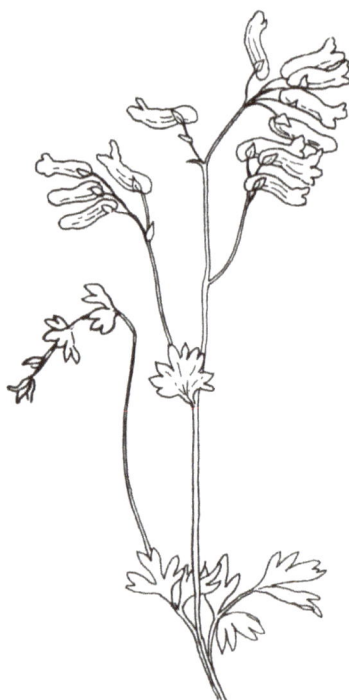

SYNONYM *Corydalis sempervirens*
Biennial herb from a fleshy taproot. **Flowers** rose to purplish, with yellow tips, spurred; several in a loose raceme. **Stems** erect (about 1 foot), glaucous, often branched. **Leaves** blue-green, pinnate (2-3), with ovate divisions, alternate on stem, an attractive leaf.

Open woods, thickets, usually in disturbed soil.

AK YT

Corydalis arctica

FEW-FLOWER CORYDALIS

SYNONYM *Corydalis pauciflora*

Perennial herb from a tuberous root. **Flowers** lavender-blue or pink, small, spurred, 1–4 flowers terminal on stem. **Stems** erect (to 6 inches), single, slender, unbranched, succulent, from a tuberous root. **Leaves** 3-parted, each lobe again divided into elongated segments, very attractive, gray-green; leaves sparse and all basal.

Moist places in arctic and alpine tundra.

AK YT

197 ■

SUE CARNAHAN

MICHAEL STITES

SUE CARNAHAN

Corydalis aurea

GOLDEN CORYDALIS

Annual or biennial herb from a taproot. **Flowers** butter-yellow, like small bleeding heart with one outer spurred petal; in loose racemes. **Stems** lax (6–8 inches), much branched, glabrous. **Leaves** grayish green, fern-like, 2–3 pinnate, drooping, alternate up stem.

Dry, roadside sands and gravels, open woods, hillsides.

AK YT

ALEKSEY BAUSHEV

ILYA RUDENKO

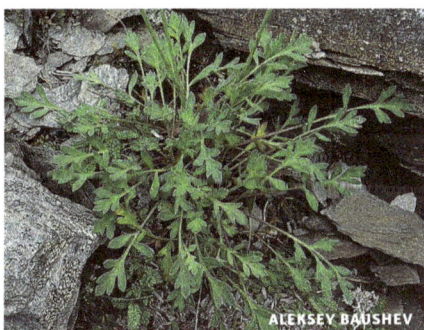

ALEKSEY BAUSHEV

Papaver lapponicum

ARCTIC POPPY

SYNONYM *Papaver radicatum*
Perennial herb from a taproot. **Flowers** lemon-yellow, or occasionally white, pale peach-color, or almost orange, with rather flat, disk-like center; petals 4, large, broadly ovate, crinkly. **Stems** erect (4–12 inches), leafless, gray-hairy. **Leaves** pinnately dissected, all basal, gray-green, hairy on both sides, tufted at base of stem.

Dry gravelly soils, tundra.

AK YT

199 ◼

DARRIN GOBBLE

BC ISLANDER

SIMONE

Erythranthe guttata

YELLOW MONKEYFLOWER

SYNONYM *Mimulus guttatus*
Annual herb from fibrous roots or a perennial from a creeping stolon. **Flowers** butter-
yellow, on peduncles from axils, 3–4 in a
group; petals 5, the lower brown-spotted.
Stems erect (to 18 inches), solitary. **Leaves**
oval, usually with toothed edge, about 4 opposite pairs sessile on stem, lower leaves
petioled.

The leaves are edible, either raw or
cooked.

Streambanks, lakeshores, ditches, seeps.

AK YT

■ 200

LAURALASKA66

VALERIA KOVALEVA

NOLAN EXE

Lagotis glauca

WEASELSNOUT

Perennial herb from a rhizome. **Flowers** bluish, small, each one in the axil of a leafy bract; these form a long, oval, compact, terminal spike. **Stems** erect (to 16 inches), stout and coarse, with small leaves on stem near flower head. **Leaves** wide, oval leaf on long petiole, heavy mid-rib, edge slightly scalloped, fleshy, form a basal, rosette-like group.

Tundra, heathlands, moist rock outcrops.

AK YT

DIETER SCHULTEN

Linaria vulgaris

BUTTER-AND-EGGS, COMMON TOADFLAX

Introduced perennial herb from a long rhizome. **Flowers** orange and yellow, spurred, snapdragon type, in a dense terminal head. **Stems** erect, to 2 feet tall, slender, wiry, smooth. **Leaves** narrow, grass-like, alternate, smooth, gray-green.

A weed of roadsides and waste places, especially near urban areas.

AK YT

ROB FOSTER

ROB FOSTER

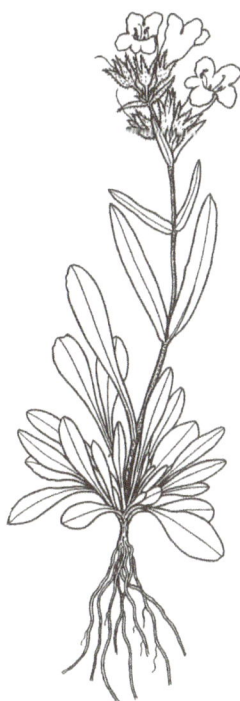

JACK BINDERNAGEL

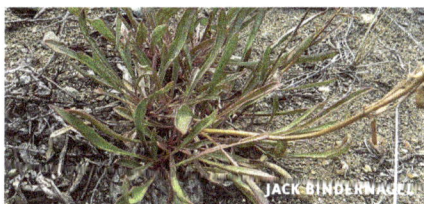

Penstemon gormanii

GORMAN'S PENSTEMON

Perennial herb from a woody base and tap-root. **Flowers** purplish or pinkish, rarely white; 2-lipped, the upper lip 2-lobed, the lower lip 3-lobed, the lobes hairy inside; in a leafy-bracted, terminal cluster of several whorls of stalked flowers; fertile stamens 4, the anthers horseshoe-shaped, smooth; the sterile stamen bearded more than half its length. **Stems** ascending to erect (to about 12 inches), several, tufted. **Leaves** opposite, mostly entire; basal leaves with petioles, smooth; stem leaves narrower, sessile, the upper leaves somewhat glandular-hairy.

Dry rocky slopes, sandy or gravelly river terraces, cut-banks.

AK YT

203 ■

MARTINE LAPOINTE

MATT BERGER

Plantago maritima

SEASIDE PLANTAIN

Perennial, taprooted herb. **Flowers** brownish-yellow, inconspicuous, densely crowded in a long terminal head. **Stems** erect (10 inches), naked, rising above the leaves. **Leaves** grass-like, long, narrow, fleshy, all from base of plant.

Eaten as a green.

Coastal marshes.

Great Plantain, *Plantago major,* an introduced perennial, weedy herb, has broadly ovate, parallel-veined leaves, and is found in waste places of the region (*not illus.*).

AK YT

SIMONE

SHAAN AROESTE

IAN ADAMS

AK | YT

Veronica americana

AMERICAN-BROOKLIME

Perennial herb from a shallow rhizome. **Flowers** blue, small, in small racemes, terminal and from leaf axils; petals 4. **Stems** lax, trailing (3-6 inches), fleshy, leafy. **Leaves** lanceolate, glabrous and somewhat succulent, margins somewhat serrate.

Shores, marshes, seeps, springs.

205 ■

DAVID ANDERSON

LOUIS IMBEAU

MANDY HACKNEY

Veronica serpyllifolia

THYME-LEAF SPEEDWELL

Perennial herb from a creeping rhizome. **Flowers** light blue with darker blue stripes, in a loose terminal cluster of 5–6 flowers; petals 4. **Stems** decumbent, (about 6 inches), rooting at nodes, much branched and mat-like, the flowering stem curves upward to seem erect. **Leaves** oval to round, tiny, in opposite pairs, sessile on stem; lower leaves on small petioles.

Moist soil along streams, seeps, swamps, roadside ditches.

AK YT

TIMOTHY MCNITT

SANDY ROBERTSON

JACK BINDERNAGEL

Veronica wormskjoldii

ALPINE SPEEDWELL

Perennial herb from a creeping rhizome.
Flowers bluish-purple, in a small, dense
terminal raceme, this elongates in fruit;
petals 4, tiny. **Stems** erect (to 12 inches),
fleshy, slightly hairy, leafy, solitary. **Leaves**
oval-pointed, sessile in opposite pairs along
stem.

Tundra, heathlands, meadows.

AK YT

ROB FOSTER

JACK BINDERNAGEL

COLE WOLF

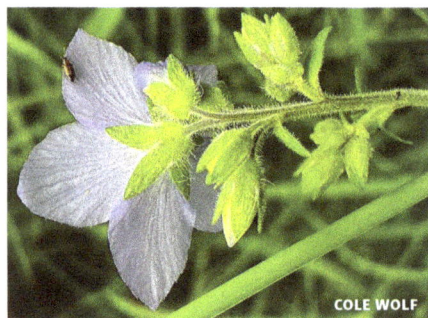

Polemonium acutiflorum

TALL JACOB'S-LADDER

Perennial herb from a rhizome. **Flowers** purplish blue with whitish centers, slightly bell-like; in an open, terminal cluster; petals 5, somewhat pointed. **Stems** erect (to 2 feet), stout, somewhat fuzzy near flowers. **Leaves** pinnately compound, alternate, with few leaves on stem; leaflets about 21, narrowly ovate and slightly pointed.

Plants show great variation in height, size and numbers of flowers.

Moist grassy places, streambanks.

AK | YT

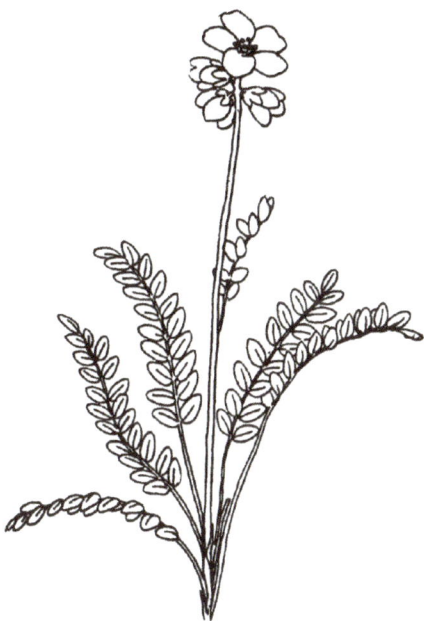

Polemonium boreale

NORTHERN JACOB'S-LADDER

Perennial herb from a rhizome. **Flowers** pale purple-lavender, with yellow at base; a dozen or so in a rather compact terminal head; petals 5 rounded. **Stems** usually erect (6–8 inches), rather stout, branched, hairy and sticky, often reddish. **Leaves** on petioles from root, pinnate; usually fewer than 21 leaflets, these rather good-sized, long oval, pointed, somewhat crowded, hairy.

Plant has a tufted appearance, most leaves rising from the root; terminal leaflets often not completely separated.

Flowers rather early (late-May, June). Arctic and alpine tundra, heathlands.

AK **YT**

209 ■

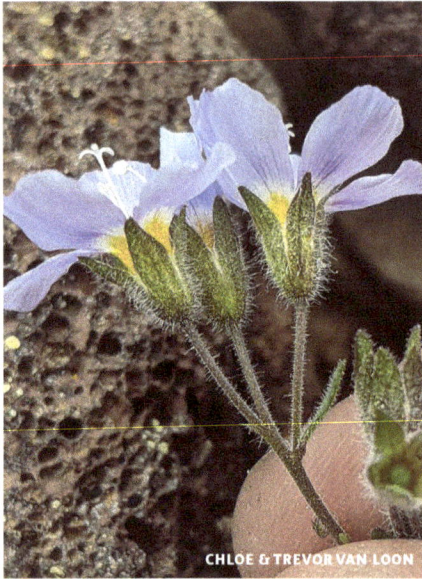

CHLOE & TREVOR VAN LOON

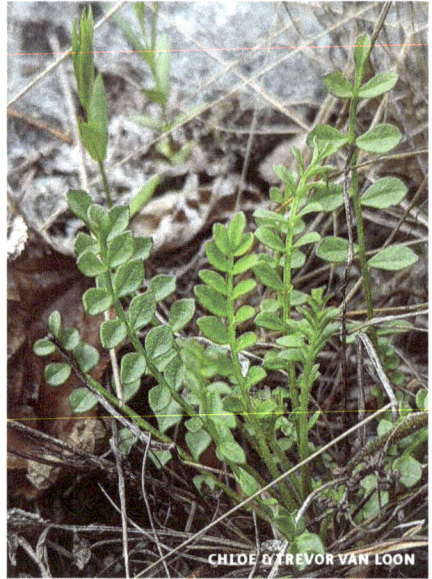

CHLOE & TREVOR VAN LOON

JACK BINDERNAGEL

Polemonium pulcherrimum

BEAUTIFUL JACOB'S-LADDER

Perennial herb from a branched base atop a taproot. **Flowers** dark purplish blue, yellow at base, funnel-shaped; on slender, long pedicels, in a loose, branched cyme; petals 5. **Stems** erect (about 1 foot), branched and spreading, with some stem leaves. **Leaves** pinnate; leaflets 21 or more, small, rounded, broad, crowded.

Appears to grow in much the same type of dry, sandy soils as *Polemonium boreale* but to flower somewhat later in season.

Open woods, meadows, roadsides, often in gravelly soils.

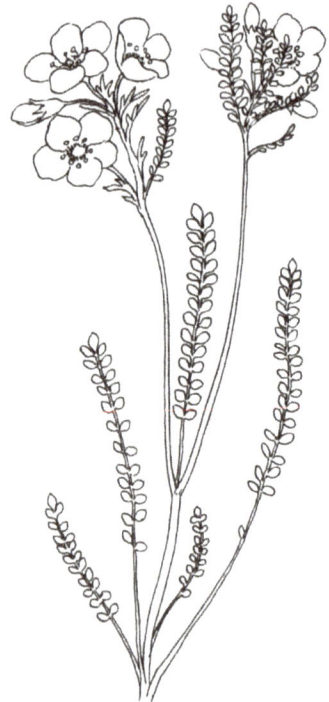

AK YT

ROB FOSTER

AERIN JACOB

ILYA RUDENKO

Bistorta plumosa

MEADOW BISTORT

SYNONYM *Polygonum bistorta*

Perennial herb with a thick hard, often contorted rhizome. **Flowers** pink to rose, tiny, densely crowded on a long terminal spike. **Stems** erect (6–12 inches), solitary, smooth and fleshy. **Leaves** broadly oval, on a long petiole, dark green above, grayish below; basal leaves usually two.

The leaves and roots are edible.

Moist alpine and arctic tundra, heathlands.

AK YT

211 ◼

LOUIS IMBEAU

INGVILD RISKA

Bistorta vivipara

ALPINE BISTORT

SYNONYM *Polygonum viviparum*
Perennial herb with a thick hard, often contorted rhizome. **Flowers** white (sometimes pink-tinged), tiny, crowded on slender spike; blossoming first at tip, the closed lower buds are pinkish. **Stems** erect (to 18 inches), solitary, slender, smooth. **Leaves** linear-lanceolate; stem leaves very slender and sharply pointed, sessile; basal leaves wider and on long petioles, with prominent midribs.

A common plant of the north. The boiled roots provide a starchy food; the leaves are edible, raw or cooked.

Dry meadows, heathlands, tundra; from lowlands to alpine areas.

AK YT

■ 212

NATHAN ODGERS

LISA BENNETT

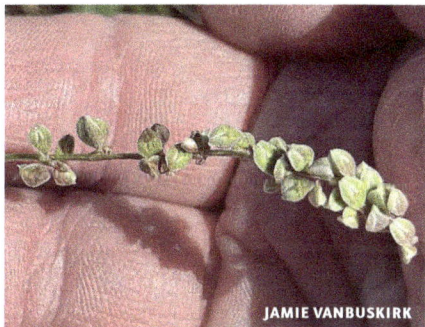

JAMIE VANBUSKIRK

Fallopia convolvulus

BLACK BINDWEED

SYNONYM *Polygonum convolvulus*
Introduced annual herb from a taproot.
Flowers greenish, small 'crumbles,' in lax
panicles from leaf axils. **Stems** trailing,
long, climbing on tall grasses. **Leaves** long,
slender arrow-shaped, pointed, on petioles,
at intervals on stems and in something of a
rosette at base of stem.

Weed of disturbed places.

AK YT

STELLA FISH

BRANDON CORDER

JANA WINBERG

Koenigia alaskana

ALASKA FLEECEFLOWER, WILD RHUBARB

SYNONYM *Polygonum alaskanum*
Perennial herb from a woody rhizome. **Flowers** creamy white, inconspicuous, many in a large, loosely branched panicle. **Stems** erect (18 inches to several feet), branched, jointed, coarse, lush. **Leaves** lanceolate, broad at base, tapering to acute point, light-green.

A tall, coarse plant. Both the leaves and the young peeled stems are eaten.

Roadsides, riverbanks, tundra.

AK YT

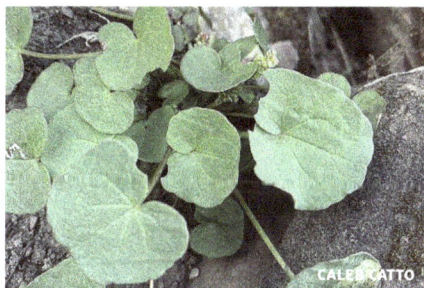

Oxyria digyna

MOUNTAIN SORREL

Perennial herb from a stout, fleshy taproot.
Flowers greenish to red, tiny, crumb-like,
in a branched panicle. **Stems** erect (4–24
inches), branched, almost leafless, from a
fleshy taproot. **Leaves** nearly round, with a
wavy margin, somewhat fleshy, on long
petioles, mostly basal; turning a reddish
color.

The fresh leaves can be eaten for a
refreshing treat while hiking.

Moist tundra, heathlands, usually where
rocky or gravelly.

AK YT

215 ■

MARTINE LAPOINTE

BENOIT RENAUD

SAM EHLERS

Persicaria lapathifolia

DOCK-LEAF SMARTWEED

SYNONYM *Polygonum lapathifolium*
Annual herb from a taproot. **Flowers** pink to white, tiny, closed; densely packed in an ovate spike-like head; flowers terminal and from upper leaf axils. **Stems** usually erect (about 1 foot), branched. **Leaves** lanceolate, very slender and long, pointed at both ends, on petioles, with a noticeable midrib.

Coarse native weed of damp roadsides, gardens, waste places.

AK YT

BREN ZO

CASSIDY BEST

ERIC LAMB

Polygonum aviculare

COMMON KNOTWEED

Annual herb from a taproot. **Flowers** pink, tiny and inconspicuous, a few in a tiny cluster from leaf axils. **Stems** decumbent, much branched (to 1 foot long). **Leaves** oval-pointed, small, alternate on stem at nodes.

A weed of waste places.

AK YT

DAN MACNEAL

SIMONE

NOAH HOW

Rumex acetosella

SHEEP SORREL

Annual or perennial herb from slender rhizomes; male and female flowers on separate plants (dioecious). **Flowers** greenish red, small, inconspicuous 'crumbles'; in small panicles, a terminal one and others from leaf axils. **Stems** erect (8-10 inches), branched, somewhat succulent, rising from a creeping rhizome. **Stem leaves** simple, linear; **basal leaves** often arrowhead-shaped, on short petioles; turning red later in season; sour to taste.

A colorful, introduced perennial.

Roadsides, abandoned fields, disturbed places.

AK YT

NPS, JACOB W. FRANK

ALEXANDRIA WENNINGER

ILYA RUDENKO

Rumex arcticus

ARCTIC DOCK

Perennial herb from a stout, fleshy rhizome. **Flowers** greenish to purplish, very small and inconspicuous, crowded on a tall, branched, panicle; seed flat and purplish red. **Stems** erect (to 4 feet), branched, stout, coarse, often reddish purple. **Leaves** long, slender, pointed; basal leaves somewhat wider and longer, with petioles.

The sour leaves are eaten both cooked and fresh in salads.

Peaty tundra, wet woods.

AK YT

Androsace chamaejasme

SWEET-FLOWER ROCK-JASMINE

Perennial, mat-forming herb. **Flowers** white (occasionally pink or lavender), with yellow eye, in small terminal umbel; petals 5, small; very fragrant. **Stems** erect (2 inches), leafless, softly hairy. **Leaves** tiny, oblanceolate, pointed, hairy, in a basal rosette.

Tundra, heathlands, often where rocky or gravelly.

AK YT

MATT BERGER

ALAN ROCKEFELLER

MY-LAN LE

Androsace septentrionalis

PYGMY-FLOWER ROCK-JASMINE

Annual or biennial, taprooted herb. **Flowers** tiny, pinkish white, one to many in a terminal cluster. **Stem** naked, wiry. **Leaves** all in a basal rosette.

Sandy and gravelly soils, rocky tundra slopes.

AK YT

KONSTANTIN SELIVERRESTOV

Y. LIU

Lysimachia europaea

ARCTIC STARFLOWER

SYNONYM *Trientalis europaea*

Perennial herb from a slender rhizome or surface runner. **Flowers** white or pinkish, usually solitary at stem end; petals 7, pointed. **Stems** erect (4–6 inches), slender, solitary, brownish green when young. **Leaves** oval, blunt, sessile, brown-green when young; the leaves in a whorl just below the blossom are the larger.

Moist woods, subalpine slopes, usually in shade.

AK YT

Primula cuneifolia

PIXIE-EYES

Tiny perennial herb from fibrous roots. **Flowers** bright magenta with a yellow 'eye,' solitary, bell-like, upright; large for the size of the plant; petals 5, notched. **Stems** erect (1 inch), elongating later in season. **Leaves** wedge-shaped, fleshy, all basal, in a tuft; margins with 5–9 large teeth.

Rocky alpine tundra, often blooming near the edge of the snow.

AK

Primula frigida

NORTHERN SHOOTINGSTAR

SYNONYM *Dodecatheon frigidum*
Perennial herb from a rhizome. **Flowers** purplish rose, with yellow 'eye,' several on pedicels, terminal on stem; petals 5, turned-back with protruding anthers. **Stems** erect (6–10 inches), slender, naked, brownish green. **Leaves** broad, long, pointed, with very long petiole, somewhat wavy-edged, all basal.

Moist tundra, meadows, woods.

AK YT

MARK POLLOCK

CALEB CATTO

Primula pauciflora

DARK-THROAT SHOOTINGSTAR

SYNONYM *Dodecatheon pulchellum*
Perennial herb from fibrous roots. **Flowers** bright magenta, with yellow 'eye;' from one to many on pedicels, terminal on naked stem; petals 5, turned-back, with protruding anthers. **Stems** erect (12–15 inches), slender, brownish green, smooth. **Leaves** broadly lanceolate, long, round-ended, simple, thick, with slender petiole, all basal.

Wet meadows.

To distinguish this species and Northern Shootingstar, in Dark-Throat Shootingstar, the filament tube is exposed, extending outwards from the surrounding anthers, and its leaves are elliptic, gradually tapered to a narrow petiole. In Northern Shootingstar the filament tube is not exposed, and its leaves are oval to ovate, and abruptly tapered into the petiole.

AK YT

225 ■

Aconitum delphiniifolium

MONKSHOOD

Perennial herb from a tuberous taproot. **Flowers** deep-purple, with one enlarged helmet-shaped upper sepal; flowers well-spaced on tall stem. **Stems** erect (to 3 feet), single, stout. **Leaves** large, palmate, cleft into 3–7 divisions, the segments long, slender, pointed.

A tall, graceful plant but poisonous (especially the seeds and roots).

Woods, meadows, tundra, subalpine slopes.

AK **YT**

IAN ADAMS

BOB WALKER

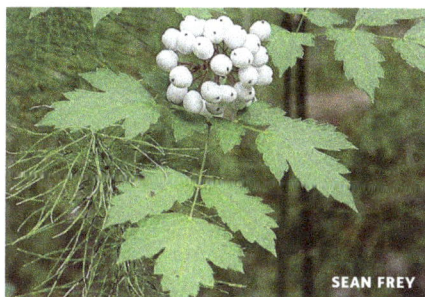
SEAN FREY

Actaea rubra

RED BANEBERRY

Perennial herb from woody base and fibrous roots. **Flowers** creamy-white, very tiny, in dense terminal branched spikes; followed by a cluster of bright red berries. **Stems** erect (to 2 feet). **Leaves** large, lacy, twice compound, thin, coarsely toothed.

Berries highly poisonous.

Plants with white fruit, formerly treated as a separate species (*Actaea alba*), are now grouped with *Actaea rubra*, and are found in about the same habitats.

Woods, open slopes, streambanks.

AK YT

227 ∎

CHLOE AND TREVOR VAN LOON

MATT BOWSER

Anemonastrum richardsonii

YELLOW ANEMONE

SYNONYM *Anemone richardsonii*
Perennial herb from a slender rhizome.
Flowers butter-yellow, solitary; petals 6.
Stems erect (3 to 8 inches), slender, wiry.
Leaves 3–5-parted, rounded but notched, somewhat hairy, one pair midway on flower stem; few, if any, basal leaves.

The first wildflower of spring in Cook Inlet area (mid-May).

Moist woods, arctic and alpine tundra.

AK YT

AERIN JACOB

MARIA KHOREVA

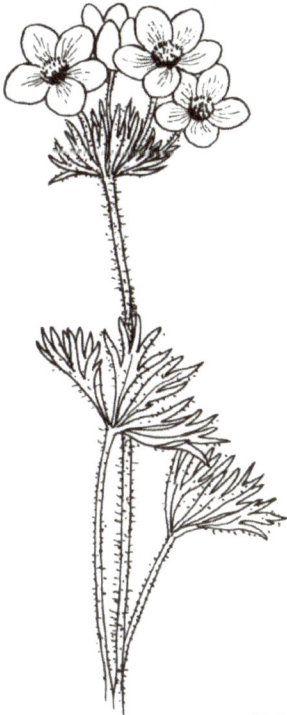

Anemonastrum sibiricum

SIBERIAN THIMBLEWEED

SYNONYM *Anemone narcissiflora*
Tufted perennial herb from a thick rhizome.
Flowers white with noticeable yellow centers, 1 inch in diameter; several in a loose
umbel at stem end. **Stems** erect (6–10
inches), rather coarse, usually hairy. **Leaves**
generally pentagonal in outline, much divided, mostly basal on long petioles; with a
group of smaller, sessile leaves just below
flower cluster.

Hybridizes freely and is variable, depending on area found.

Subalpine open woods, arctic and alpine
tundra, heathlands.

AK | YT

229 ■

MY-LAN LE

EZEQUIEL RACKER

TODD BOLAND

Anemone multifida

WINDFLOWER

Perennial herb from a woody base. **Flowers** white, sometimes blue or pink on the back, solitary, about 1 inch in diameter; petals 5. **Stems** erect (6–8 inches), slender, slightly hairy. **Leaves** broad, one or two times 3-parted, hairy; mostly basal with one pair high on flower stem.

    Gravelly slopes, open woods, meadows, roadsides.

AK YT

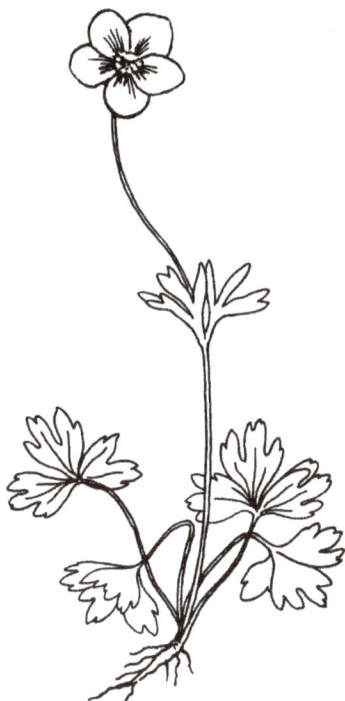

Anemone parviflora

SMALL-FLOWER ANEMONE

Perennial herb from a woody base and slender rhizomes. **Flowers** white (often tinged with blue or pink on the back), usually solitary and large in proportion to total plant; petals 5. **Stems** erect, short, unbranched, silky at base. **Leaves** 3-parted with blunt teeth, smooth, dark green, on long petioles, mostly basal, but with one pair of sessile stem leaves.

Moist woods, arctic and alpine tundra, heathlands.

AK | YT

TODD BOLAND

LAUREN MARKEWICZ

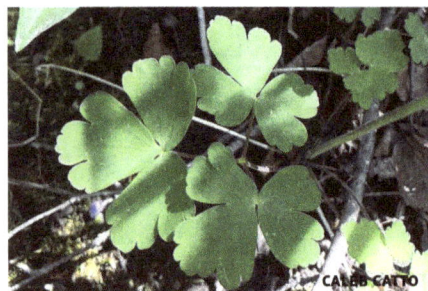
CALEB CATTO

Aquilegia brevistyla

SMALL-FLOWER COLUMBINE

Perennial herb from a taproot. **Flowers** dark-blue, creamy white inside, nodding; petals 5, prolonged into small, rounded spurs. **Stems** erect (8–15 inches), slender, branched, somewhat silky, with a few small, nearly sessile, stem leaves. **Leaves** twice 3-lobed, shallowly scalloped, mostly basal on petioles.

Flowers and plants smaller than in Crimson Columbine (*Aquilegia formosa*).

Moist woods, meadows, gravelly soils.

AK YT

TIMOTHY MCNITT

TIMOTHY MCNITT

SUBIR B. SHAKYA

Aquilegia formosa

CRIMSON COLUMBINE

Perennial herb from a woody base and a taproot. **Flowers** lacquer-red, yellow inside, the 5 petals are prolonged backward into acute spurs; on long peduncles. **Stems** erect (to 4 feet), branching, wiry, brownish red. **Leaves** 2-times 3-parted, the attractive leaflets round-ovate, cleft, glaucous.

A beautiful and plentiful roadside flower in the Matanuska Valley, on the Kenai, near Haines and Valdez, and even up into the Talkeetna Mountains.

Open woods, heathlands.

AK YT

JOHN A HASKINS

MATT BERGER

ALAN ROCKEFELLER

Caltha leptosepala

WHITE MARSH-MARIGOLD

Perennial herb from a thick base with fibrous roots. **Flowers** white, large with a yellow center; petals 8. **Stems** erect (4–6 inches). **Leaves** often solitary, heart-shaped, simple, fleshy, on long petioles, often all basal.

Mountain streambanks, moist heath.

AK YT

■ 234

HKNUETTEL

MICHAEL NEWLON

Caltha palustris

YELLOW MARSH-MARIGOLD

Perennial herb from a thick base with fibrous roots. **Flowers** deep-yellow, large, often several in a terminal cluster; petals 5. **Stems** partially decumbent (to 15 inches), fleshy, hollow, branched, sometimes with a reddish tinge. **Leaves** large, kidney-shaped with fine teeth on margins, shiny dark green; basal leaves on petioles, leaves on stems somewhat clasping.

Very showy and attractive, variable depending on locality. Leaves and stems are cooked and eaten as greens; raw leaves are poisonous.

Wet shores, marshes, streams, often in shallow water.

AK **YT**

CRICKET RASPET

VELODROME

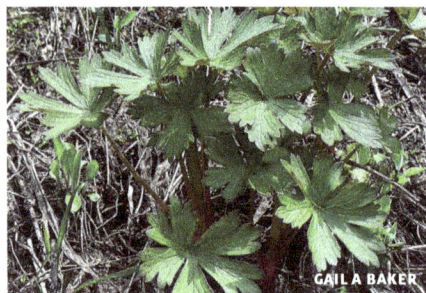

GAIL A BAKER

Delphinium glaucum

SIERRA LARKSPUR

Perennial herb from a thick rootstock.
Flowers deep blue-purple; irregularly
shaped, with one spurred petal; flowers
smaller than in the cultivated delphinium,
sparsely spaced out on a very tall spike.
Stems erect (to 6 feet), brownish green,
stout, hollow. **Leaves** large, palmately cleft,
with deeply toothed segments, alternate;
mostly basal with a few stem leaves.

Poisonous.

Moist grassy places, thickets, streambanks, from sea-level to higher elevations.

AK YT

■ 236

JACK BINDERNAGEL

CHRISTINA NGUYEN

Pulsatilla nuttalliana

PASQUEFLOWER

SYNONYM *Anemone patens*
Tufted perennial from a stout ascending
rhizome. **Flowers** deep-lavender with yellow centers, large; followed by long feathery
styles, very attractive, even in fruit; petals 6.
Stems erect (to 8 inches), very silky, sometimes branched. **Leaves** rather small, much
cleft, very hairy, and often folded and not
fully open; one small pair is sessile on
flower stem.

One of the very earliest spring flowers in
central Alaska and the Yukon, and one of
the handsomest of any season.

Arctic and alpine tundra, soils often
sandy.

AK   YT

237 ■

KEN CLARK

VLADIMIR ATACHKIN

CHRISTIAN BERG

Ranunculus acris

TALL BUTTERCUP

Perennial herb from fibrous roots, sometimes with rhizomes. **Flowers** deep-yellow, shiny, solitary, on pedicels; petals 5, rounded; sepals hairy. **Stems** erect (to 2 feet), branched, slightly hairy, with a few leaves. **Leaves** palmately divided (3–7 lobes), each cut into three, linear segments, somewhat hairy; the basal leaves with petioles.

All species of *Ranunculus* should be considered poisonous and never eaten.

Meadows, roadsides.

AK YT

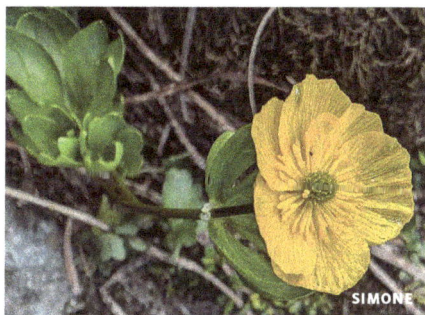

Ranunculus eschscholtzii

ESCHSCHOLTZ'S BUTTERCUP

Perennial herb from a compact base. **Flowers** butter-yellow, large, with conelike center, 1–3 on a stem; petals 5. **Stems** erect (6–8 inches), smooth. **Leaves** broad, 3–5-parted and cleft, mostly basal, with one pair on stem.

A handsome plant which resembles a lush anemone, except for the cone-like flower centers.

Moist alpine meadows, streambanks.

AK YT

MATT BERGER

MATT BERGER

TIMOTHY MCNITT

Ranunculus flammula

CREEPING SPEARWORT

SYNONYM *Ranunculus reptans*

Perennial herb, usually with stolons. **Flowers** yellow, small, 6-petaled, one or two from stem ends. **Stems** decumbent, slender, rooting at nodes, partially floating when growing in water, flower stems erect. **Leaves** grass-like, very slender and long, basal leaves tufted.

Wet or muddy shores, shallow ponds.

AK YT

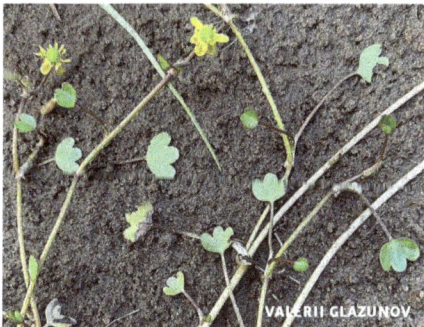

Ranunculus hyperboreus

ARCTIC BUTTERCUP

Perennial herb. **Flowers** yellow, with a very prominent cone-like center; petals 5 tiny. **Stems** decumbent, trailing (2–12 inches), branched, fleshy but slender and smooth; rooting at nodes. **Leaves** three-lobed, fleshy, small, blunt, sometimes further divided into 3 segments.

Shallow ponds, mud flats, shores.

AK **YT**

241 ∎

NICOLE

NICOLE

DOMINIC GENTILCORE

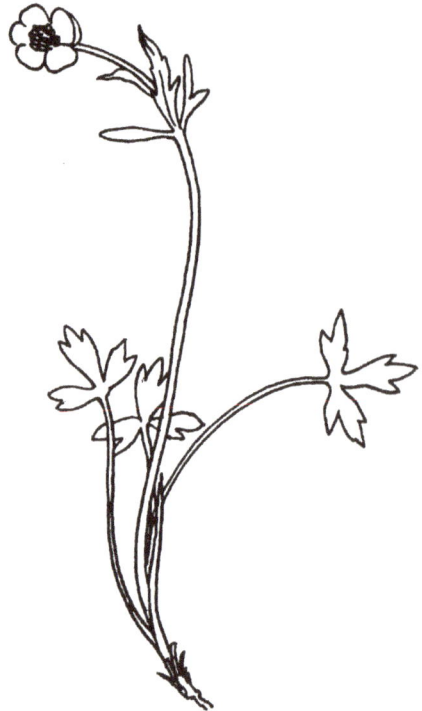

Ranunculus occidentalis

WESTERN BUTTERCUP

Perennial herb from a cluster of fibrous roots. **Flowers** butter-yellow, medium-sized, solitary, terminal on a peduncle from a cluster of leafy bracts. **Stems** erect (6–8 inches), slender, leafless, smooth. **Leaves** few, light-green glossy, on long petioles from root, 3-lobed, each lobe with 3 sharply cut, pointed segments.

Alpine meadows, tundra.

AK YT

THOMAS KOFFEL

BRANDON CORDER

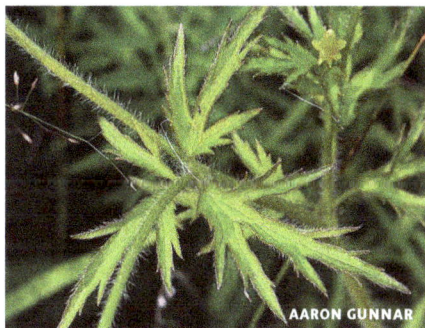

AARON GUNNAR

Ranunculus pensylvanicus

BRISTLY BUTTERCUP

Annual or short-lived perennial herb from a cluster of fibrous roots. **Flowers** yellow, small, with a bristly conelike center, in open cymes; petals 5. **Stems** erect (12 inches or more), branched, hairy. **Leaves** 3-parted, and cleft again several times, with very sharp, toothed margins.

Weedy in moist disturbed places, meadows.

AK

243 ∎

NATHAN AARON

SALTYHIKER

IVAN SHIKHALEV

Ranunculus sceleratus

CURSED CROWFOOT

Annual herb, from slender, fleshy roots. **Flowers** yellow, rather small but with very prominent conelike centers, terminal and from leaf axils. **Stems** erect (about 8 inches), fleshy, branched, smooth. **Leaves** 3-parted and divided again into 3 blunt lobes, on long petioles, glabrous.

Shallow ponds, muskegs, mud flats, roadside ditches.

AK YT

MATT BERGER

JONATHAN CURLEY

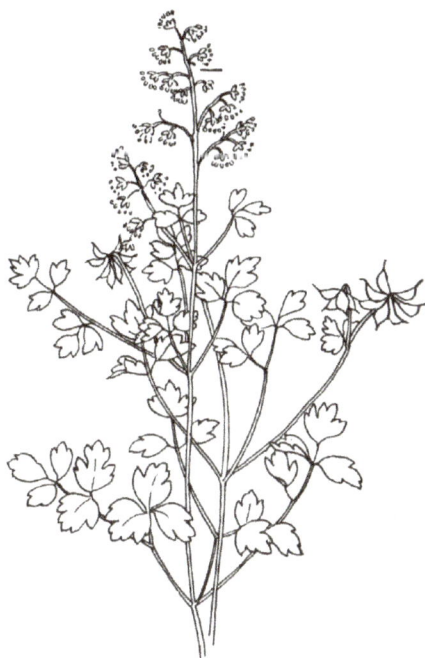

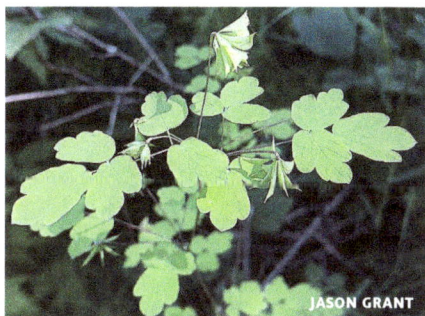
JASON GRANT

Thalictrum sparsiflorum

FEW-FLOWER MEADOW-RUE

Perennial herb from a rhizome. **Flowers** greenish white, very tiny, calyx red-brown, a very few in a small cluster; followed by groups of small, flat, brown seeds. **Stems** erect (to 3 feet), branched, brownish green, smooth, leafy. **Leaves** 3 times compound, thin, delicate; an attractive small leaf which somewhat resembles those of the columbine.

Woods, meadows, thickets.

AK YT

245 ■

LOGAN J.L. BRADLEY

ALAN ROCKEFELLER

MERLLA MCLAUGHLIN

Amelanchier alnifolia

SASKATOON, SERVICEBERRY

Shrub, or less often a small tree. **Flowers** white, in loose racemes, followed by a blue-black, juicy berry in July; petals 5. **Stems** woody (to 16 feet). **Leaves** small, smooth, oval, alternate, thick and firm, toothed near tip. **Fruits** dull red at first, becoming purple to nearly black, sweet and edible but the seed is quite large.

Open woods, dry rocky slopes.

AK YT

BRYN

WOLFGANG AHLMER

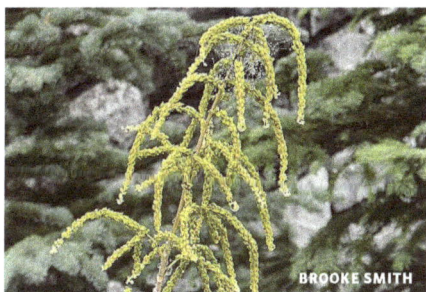

BROOKE SMITH

Aruncus dioicus

GOAT'S-BEARD

Large perennial herb from stout rhizome. **Flowers** creamy-white, tiny, closed, in very large branched panicles. **Stems** erect (4–5 feet), brownish green when young, stout. **Leaves** large, 2–3 times pinnate with large, toothed leaflets, often brownish when young.

This attractive perennial blossoms early in the valleys (June, July).

Moist woods, meadows, streambanks; not found far from the coast.

AK

247 ■

TODD BOLAND

PIETER HUYBRECHTS

MAUREEN_C-M

Comarum palustre

MARSH CINQUEFOIL

SYNONYM *Potentilla palustris*
Medium shrub from creeping rootstock.
Flowers deep red-brown, in small groups
terminal on stem or in leaf axils, with defi-
nite conelike center; petals 5, pointed; calyx
lobes longer than petals. **Stems** erect (to
about 2 feet), stout, branched, somewhat
hairy. **Leaves** 5–7 lobed, the lobes sharply
toothed; with small, simple leaflets in
flower heads.

Wet places, bogs, roadside ditches,
streambanks, often in shallow water.

AK YT

CALEB CATTO

RACHEL STRINGHAM

Dasiphora fruticosa

SHRUBBY CINQUEFOIL, TUNDRA ROSE

SYNONYM *Potentilla fruiticosa*
Low to medium-sized shrub. **Flowers** butter-yellow, solitary, petals 5. **Stems** erect (to 3 feet), much-branched, brown. **Leaves** 5-parted: two pairs of narrow pointed leaflets with a terminal leaflet somewhat wider and more blunt; smooth, bright dark-green above, whitish on underside, a noticeably attractive leaf.

One of the first flowers seen in Alaska at the Yukon border in June or July, and a much-beloved plant in Alaska.

Tundra, bogs, alpine slopes, in wet to dry places.

AK YT

249 ■

CHLOE & TREVOR VAN LOON

AKR

Dryas drummondii

YELLOW MOUNTAIN-AVENS

Prostrate shrub from a thick woody base; stems trailing, branching and rooting, mat-forming, often forming large colonies. **Flowers** yellow, solitary, nodding; petals 6; the styles become attractively feathery after the petals are shed. **Flower stems** erect (4–6 inches), slender, leafless. **Leaves** shaped like an oak leaf, but slender, with irregular and somewhat turned back margins, rounded tips, on petioles, whitish underneath, mostly basal.

　　Dry gravelly floodplains, terraces, river bars, at various elevations.

AK YT

■ 250

AKR

LAURA MASKELL

AK YT

PAUL PRIOR

Dryas integrifolia

WHITE MOUNTAIN-AVENS

Prostrate shrub from a woody base; stems trailing, branching and rooting, forming dense mats. **Flowers** white with golden center, about 1 inch in diameter, solitary. **Flower stems** erect (about 6 inches), fuzzy. **Leaves** on petioles, crowded on the woody stem; the margins entire or with a few teeth on the lower half, often rolled under.

Arctic and alpine tundra, heath, gravelly alpine ridges.

Another *Dryas*, **Alaska Mountain-Avens** (*Dryas alaskensis*, ILLUS., LEFT) is also common in the region, and includes plants formerly classified as *Dryas octopetala*. It has white flowers and its leaves are toothed on the margins.

VIRGINIA HUDSON

Alaska Mountain-Avens
(*Dryas alaskensis*)

251

INSPECTAHJESS

LÉO-GUY DE REPENTIGNY

CORY CHIAPPONE

Fragaria virginiana

WILD STRAWBERRY

Perennial herb from a fibrous root, with sur-face runners. **Flowers** white in an open cluster; petals 5. **Stems** trailing, rooting at the nodes. **Leaves** palmately compound, leaflets 3, the margins coarsely toothed, the terminal tooth less than 1/2 as wide as and shorter than the adjacent teeth. **Fruit** a small, delicious strawberry, ripening in late July and August.

Fields, clearings, open hillsides at low-elevations.

AK YT

RM123

CORY CHIAPPONE

GENITA NOLAN

Geum macrophyllum

LARGE-LEAF AVENS

Perennial herb from a stout base and short rhizome. **Flowers** light-yellow; petals 5, surrounding a prominent center of hooked styles; after the petals are shed a head of reddish seeds develops. **Stems** erect (to 2 feet), branched, sparsely hairy. **Leaves** large, slightly hairy, shallowly pinnate, with a large terminal leaflet which is rounded and three-cleft; margins somewhat toothed.

Open woods, wet meadows, beaches, roadsides.

AK **YT**

253 ∎

SAGE NILES

STISHOVITE

Geum rossii

ROSS' AVENS

Perennial herb from a stout base and thick scaly rhizome. **Flowers** deep butter-yellow, shining, 1 inch wide, 1–2 on stem; petals 5; calyx hairy. **Stems** erect, (4–6 inches), a few small leaflets on stem. **Leaves** from base very attractive, pinnate, (up to 15 leaflets), each leaflet notched, with the terminal segment the largest; petioles rise from rootstock.

Wet alpine areas, often close to snow.

ADDITIONAL SPECIES

Caltha-Leaf Avens (*Geum calthifolium*, ILLUS., RIGHT) a perennial herb with a single yellow flower, and large, rounded, slightly toothed basal leaves, is found in moist alpine meadows in coastal areas of Alaska (absent from the Yukon).

`AK` `YT`

STISHOVITE

■ 254

TIMOTHY MCNITT

DOMINIC GENTILCORE

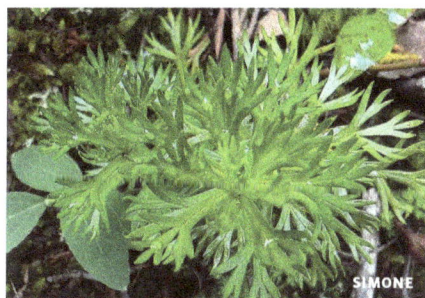

SIMONE

Luetkea pectinata

PARTRIDGEFOOT

SYNONYM *Saxifraga pectinata*
Prostrate, mat-forming, semi-shrub from a
creeping rhizome and stolons. **Flowers**
creamy-white, in erect racemes; petals 5,
very small. **Stems** erect (3-4 inches).
Leaves very feathery and much-divided,
attractive, in various shades of green,
crowded at base of stem; from a distance,
resembling a moss.

Subalpine heaths, alpine slopes; roadsides in the Talkeetna Mountains are car-
peted with this in July.

AK YT

255 ■

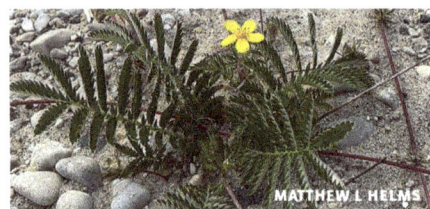

Potentilla anserina

SILVERWEED

SYNONYM *Argentina anserina*
Perennial herb from long, stolons (straw-berry-like runners). **Flowers** yellow, soli-tary on long pedicels; petals 5. **Flowering stems** erect (4–5 inches), slender, some-what hairy. **Leaves** pinnate, deeply cut, fern-like, with up to 30 toothed leaflets, smooth green above, white-silky under-neath, all basal and forming something of a tuft.

Unlike the shiny yellow petals of the but-tercups (*Ranunculus*), *Potentilla* petals are a duller yellow.

Sandy beaches, tidal flats, shores, road-sides.

AK YT

Potentilla biflora

TWO-FLOWER CINQUEFOIL

Small perennial herb from a branched base. **Flowers** lemon-yellow, single, petals 5; flowers large for size of plant. **Flower stems** erect (to 4 inches), silky. **Leaves** 3-parted, with large linear leaflets, the terminal leaflet cut nearly to its base, on long petioles, hairy on underside; rather tufted in growth, with a pair of small stem leaves near the flowers.

At higher elevations on rocky soils, heathlands, hillsides.

AK **YT**

257 ■

NAVA BRIMBLE

BRIAN STARZOMSKI

Potentilla bimundorum

CUT-LEAF CINQUEFOIL

SYNONYM *Potentilla multifida*
Perennial herb from a much-branched base.
Flowers light-yellow; in an open, branched
terminal cluster; petals 5; calyx grayish
woolly. **Stems** erect (to 15 inches), reddish,
often with several stems from one root;
young plants are decumbent. **Leaves** pinnately dissected into about 7 leaflets, those
nearest petiole are mere whiskers, others
cut into linear divisions nearly to their base;
bright dark-green above, gray velvety underneath; with small, sessile leaflets near
the flower heads.

Dry slopes, gravel bars, scree slopes.

AK **YT**

■ 258

CALEB CATTO

PRAIRIEBOY

RWR

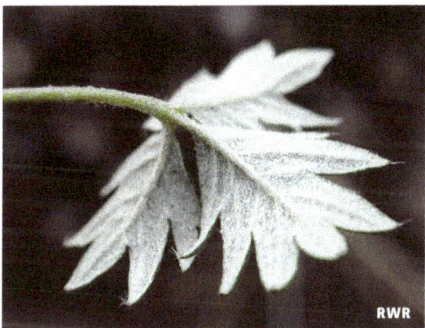

Potentilla nivea

SNOW CINQUEFOIL

Perennial herb from a short rhizome. **Flowers** butter-yellow, few in a terminal cyme; petals 5. **Stems** 6–9 inches. **Leaves** mainly basal, small, 3-parted, toothed, long-hairy beneath.

Dry open slopes, scree, roadsides; soils often gravelly and sandy.

AK YT

259 ■

OWEN CLARKIN

CORY CHIAPPONE

MICHAEL H. KING

Potentilla norvegica

ROUGH CINQUEFOIL

Annual to biennial herb from a taproot.
Flowers pale-yellow, small, a few blossoms
in a leafy terminal cluster and also from
upper leaf axils; calyx lobes longer than
petals. **Stems** erect (to 2 feet), coarse, hairy,
reddish, leafy. **Leaves** 3-lobed, leaflets
toothed, alternate on stem, on petioles,
hairy.

Old fields, roadsides, meadows.

AK **YT**

DUSTIN SNIDER

MAPLEDONUT

JACK BINDERNAGEL

Potentilla pensylvanica

PRAIRIE CINQUEFOIL

Perennial herb. **Flowers** large, deep-yellow in a terminal cyme. **Stems** (to about 2 feet), reddish. **Basal leaves** large, with 7 or more lobes, each deeply toothed, on long petioles; **stem leaves** several.

Dry mountain slopes, open woods, tundra, heathlands.

AK YT

261 ■

ANDY FYON

JOZIEN

BRIAN STARZOMSKI

Potentilla villosula

NORTHERN CINQUEFOIL

SYNONYM *Potentilla villosa*

Perennial herb. **Flowers** butter-yellow, in small terminal groups; petals 5, medium to large; sepals and the small bracts with the flowers sharply pointed and silvery gray. **Stems** erect (to 12 inches), branched and slender, without leaves. **Leaves** 3-parted, lobes almost round, toothed; gray-green on upperside, more silky below; basal, on petioles.

An attractive, gray-silky plant.
Rocky cliffs and outcrops.

AK YT

RYAN SEALY

STEVE ANSELL

SAM

Rosa acicularis

PRICKLY ROSE

Shrub, spreading by extensive rhizomes, sometimes forming thickets. **Flowers** light pink to deep-rose, with large yellow centers, fragrant, solitary and in groups; petals 5, large; followed by long-oval, fleshy 'hip.' **Stems** erect (to 4 feet), branched, prickly, brown. **Leaves** of 3–9 oval leaflets, pointed, with finely toothed edges, slightly fuzzy on underside.

The reddish fruits ("hips") are widely used in jelly-making both because of their color and for their high Vitamin C content. However, eating the spiny seeds **should be avoided** as they can irritate the stomach.

Open woods, thickets, meadows.

AK YT

263

NICOLA RAMMELL

ADAM PARRIER

CHRISTIAN GRENIER

Rubus arcticus

NAGOONBERRY, ARCTIC RASPBERRY

Perennial herb from a slender rhizome. **Flowers** deep-magenta, solitary; followed by a red to purplish raspberry-like fruit; petals 5, calyx lobes narrow. **Stems** erect (3–5 inches, taller at low elevations). **Leaves** broad, 3-parted; leaflets notched. **Fruit** a small, red, tasty berry, ripening in August, but only found in quantity in southeastern Alaska.

Moist meadows, streambanks, alpine slopes, tundra.

AK **YT**

CHRISTIAN LANGLOIS

MAUREEN_C-M

TODD BOLAND

Rubus chamaemorus

CLOUDBERRY, BAKED-APPLE BERRY

Perennial herb from a slender rhizome. **Flowers** white, solitary; followed by a soft, raspberry-like fruit, at first reddish, ripening to amber or yellow; petals 5, large. **Stems** erect (2–6 inches). **Leaves** broad, with 5 rounded, finely toothed lobes, stems usually with 2–3 leaves. **Berries** edible, with a taste reminiscent of a baked apple; ripening in August and September.

Bogs, damp peaty tundra, moist woods.

AK YT

265 ∎

PETER ANDERSEN

BOB MILLER

JACOB ROETSCHER

Rubus idaeus

COMMON RED RASPBERRY

Shrub with biennial stems (canes). **Flowers** white, in loose clusters; followed by red fruit; petals 5. **Stems** erect (2–4 feet), branched, bristly, brownish red. **Leaves** lobed into 3–5 slightly toothed segments, hairy on underside.

A delicious edible berry.

Woods, thickets, recent clearings.

AK YT

BRYN

JACK BINDERNAGEL

MARCEL_PEPIN

Rubus spectabilis

SALMONBERRY

Shrub, from extensive rhizomes, often thicket-forming. **Flowers** magenta-rose, solitary; petals 5, somewhat pointed; calyx lobes wider than in *Rubus arcticus*. **Stems** erect, branched (to about 3 feet), bristly, a shreddy-barked. **Leaves** lobed, with 3 rather broad, pointed, leaflets, all coarsely and unevenly notched; the terminal one often the largest. **Fruit** an attractive yellow, orange, or red berry, but seedy for eating fresh; however, it makes an excellent jelly.

Moist woods and thickets, mostly in coastal areas.

AK

Sanguisorba canadensis

CANADIAN BURNET

Perennial herb from a stout rhizome. **Flowers** greenish white, tiny, fragrant, with protruding stamens, forming a dense, terminal head on a bare stem; when the flowers open this head becomes compact-cylindrical. **Stems** erect (about 18 inches), stout, wiry, and somewhat leafy. **Leaves** pinnate, with usually 7, wide, blunt-ended, rather sharply toothed, rose-like leaflets, mostly basal.

Bogs, wet meadows.

AK YT

POLINA POZHALNKINA

POLINA POZHALNKINA

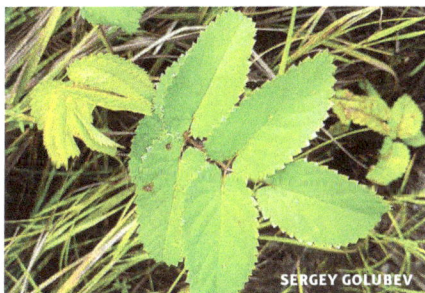

SERGEY GOLUBEV

Sanguisorba officinalis

GREAT BURNET

Perennial herb from a short rhizome. **Flowers** purplish red, tiny, forming a dense, terminal head about an inch long on a naked stem; occasionally this stem is branched and there may be 1-2 additional flower heads. **Stems** erect (12–18 inches), rigid, slender, wiry; flower stem rises well above the leaves. **Leaves** pinnate (7 or more leaflets), long-oval, blunt, evenly toothed, much like a rose leaf, chiefly basal.

Tundra, heath, woods, often in deep grass.

AK YT

269 ◾

CHLOE & TREVOR VAN LOON

VALERY KOVALEV

JARED SHORMA

Sibbaldia procumbens

CREEPING SIBBALDIA

Small, tufted, perennial herb from a shreddy woody base and rhizome. **Flowers** yellow, in cymes of 3–4; petals 5, very small. **Stems** short (4–5 inches), almost creeping. **Leaves** 3-lobed, each lobe slender, squared off at tip with 3 small teeth, on long petioles from rootstock; old leaves persisting.

Moist alpine meadows, snowbeds, open woods.

AK YT

DANIELS

DEE SHEA HIMES

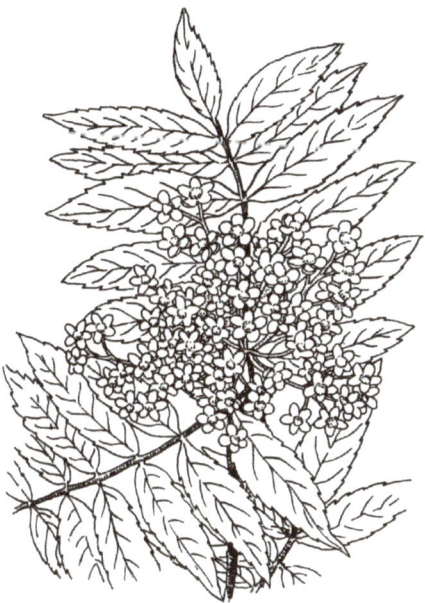

MERLLA MCLAUGHLIN

Sorbus scopulina

CASCADE MOUNTAIN-ASH

Large shrub, less often a small tree. **Flowers** white; in a terminal, branched, compound cyme, round-topped; followed by a cluster of glossy orange-red berries; petals 5 very small. **Stems** erect (10–20 feet), branched. **Leaves** alternate, pinnate with 7–17 leaflets; leaflets elliptic-lanceolate, finely toothed.

AK YT

Woods, mountain slopes, alpine tundra.

Spiraea stevenii

ALASKA SPIRAEA

SYNONYM *Spiraea beauverdiana*
Low shrub, from creeping rhizomes. **Flowers** white (pink when in bud), small, simple, in flattened clusters, very similar to the cultivated spiraea. **Stems** erect (6–24 inches), branched, slender, wiry; with smooth, reddish bark. **Leaves** ovate to oblong, rounded at ends, slightly toothed, on short petioles, pale green on underside.

A tea can be made from the leaves.
Woods, tundra, alpine slopes.

AK **YT**

CHRISTIAN BERG

ERIC LAMB

AK YT

Galium boreale

NORTHERN BEDSTRAW

Perennial herb from a rhizome. **Flowers** white, tiny; in long, open, terminal panicles; with small leaflets at each branching. **Stems** erect (to 2 feet), smooth, much-branched, four-angled. **Leaves** lanceolate, small, long, narrow, usually blunt-tipped, in whorls of four along the stem.

The name 'bedstraw' refers to the plant's former use as mattress stuffing as it has a sweet-scent when dried, and the square stems are somewhat resistant to being crushed.

Woods, tundra, roadsides.

273

T. J. SAMOJEDNY

KEN-ICHI UEDA

KEN-ICHI UEDA

Galium trifidum

THREE-PETAL BEDSTRAW

Perennial herb, often in mats. **Flowers** white, very small, on longish peduncles, in terminal clusters of usually 3 flowers. **Stems** lax, weak, branched, leafy. **Leaves** lanceolate, narrow, blunt, with a noticeable midrib, usually in whorls of four around stem.

Moist woods, bogs, swamps, pond margins, roadside ditches.

AK YT

ARCTIC WILLOW — ILYA RUDENKO

NET-VEIN WILLOW — TODD BOLAND

SKELETON-LEAF WILLOW — BRANDON CORDER

ROUND-LEAF WILLOW — JASON GRANT

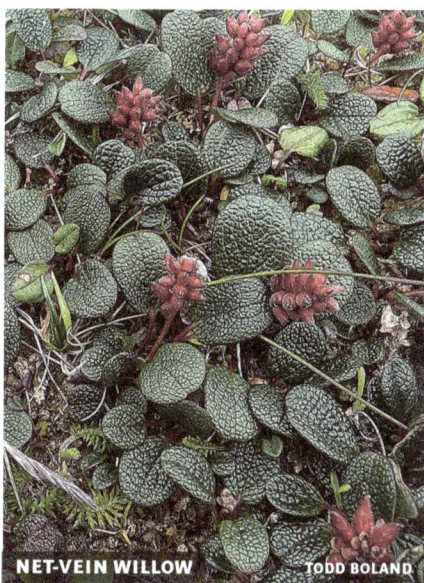

Salix reticulata

NET-VEIN WILLOW

Dwarf shrub, spreading by layering. **Flowers** grouped into catkins Also called *aments*), these either of all male or all female flowers, erect on stem, large. **Stems** (to 6 inches) creeping. **Leaves** nearly round, in whorls or small rosettes just below the catkin, gray on underside, markedly net-veined; petioles often reddish.

In this species the vegetative twigs are almost always tipped with a catkin.

Many species of *Salix,* some with attractive yellow, white, pink, or gray catkins, grow in Alaska and the Yukon; most of these are much taller shrubs or small trees.

Other common dwarf willows of the tundra are **Arctic Willow** (*Salix arctica*), **Skeleton-Leaf Willow** (*Salix phlebophylla*), and **Round-Leaf Willow** (*Salix rotundifolia*); see photographs.

Arctic and alpine tundra.

AK YT

Geocaulon lividum

FALSE TOADFLAX, TIMBERBERRY

Perennial, partially parasitic herb from spreading rhizomes. **Flowers** greenish, inconspicuous, on stem ends and in upper axils; followed by an orange-brown berry in July, something of the shape of a blueberry; petals 5, pointed. **Stems** erect (about 6 inches), slender. **Leaves** rounded oval, small, thin, brownish when young, often mottled.

Flowers very early (mid- to late-May). Berries edible but tasteless.

Tundra, open woods, may form large colonies in open birch stands.

AK YT

Chrysosplenium tetrandrum

NORTHERN GOLDEN-SAXIFRAGE

Perennial herb from slender stolons. **Flowers** greenish-yellow, cup-like with red centers, very tiny, appearing at first glance to be petals but are calyx lobes, in a small group at top of stem. **Stems** rather weak (about 4 inches), succulent, glabrous. **Leaves** rounded, shallowly scalloped, on petioles, chiefly basal, with some terminal near flowers, succulent, tender.

Wet soil or shallow water of seeps and streambanks.

AK YT

277 ■

JASON GRANT

TIMOTHY MCNITT

GABRIEL CAMPBELL

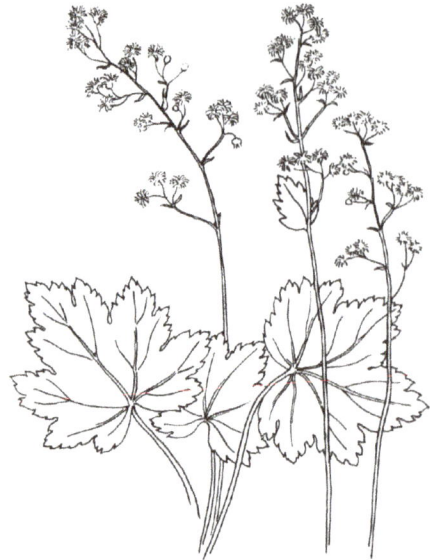

Heuchera glabra

ALPINE ALUMROOT

Perennial herb from rhizomes. **Flowers** white, tiny, scattered toward top of a tall stem in a loose raceme. **Stems** erect (to about 18 inches), slender; the panicles rising well above leaves. **Leaves** broad, 3–5-lobed, on long petioles, not unlike a small maple leaf; most leaves basal.

Moist, rocky cliffs, slopes, streambanks; coastal areas of Alaska.

AK

AIVA NORINGSETH

JOHN BREW

ALAN COVINGTON

Leptarrhena pyrolifolia

LEATHERLEAF SAXIFRAGE

Perennial herb from rhizomes. **Flowers** white, in large terminal panicle (when immature, flowers red-green in a compact terminal cluster); petals 5, small. Even by mid-July, in the mountains, flowers have been followed by bright rose-colored seed cases. **Stems** erect (12–15 inches); with 1–2 small, sessile leaves on stem. **Leaves** in basal tuft or rosette, green above, lighter on underside, spatulate, rounded at end, somewhat notched, thick, leathery, stiff, tapered to a short petiole; old leaves persistent.

Moist alpine meadows, streambanks, heathlands.

AK YT

279 ■

Micranthes hieraciifolia

STIFF-STEM SAXIFRAGE

SYNONYM *Saxifraga hieracifolia*
Tufted perennial herb. **Flowers** greenish red, tiny, in axils of tiny bracts at top of the stem. **Stems** erect (8–10 inches), fleshy and stout, leafless. **Leaves** long, diamond-shaped, wide, pointed, slightly toothed toward tip, narrowing to a short petiole, fleshy, shiny green, all basal in a rosette.

The leaves of most *Micranthes* and *Saxifraga* are edible.

Streambanks, moist tundra, alpine meadows.

AK **YT**

IAN ADAMS

MARTINE LAPOINTE

ALAN COVINGTON

Micranthes lyallii

RED-STEM SAXIFRAGE

SYNONYM *Saxifraga lyallii*
Perennial herb from rhizomes, often forming mats. **Flowers** white, small; with one to
many flowers in an open, branched panicle;
stamens red, always noticeable, remaining
after the petals fall. **Stems** erect (to 12
inches), reddish tinged, branched, leafless.
Leaves broad, fan-shaped but small, with
usually 11 notches on the rounded part of
leaf, in a basal rosette.

Snowbeds, wet places near streams and
seeps, often at high elevations.

AK YT

281 ■

ILYA FILIPPOV

ILYA RUDENKO

ILYA RUDENKO

Micranthes nelsoniana

BROOK SAXIFRAGE

SYNONYM *Saxifraga punctata*
Perennial herb from a cord-like rhizome.
Flowers white, tiny, 3-4 in a group, in an
open head; petals 5. **Stems** erect (4-20
inches), slender, leafless, often in a large
cluster. **Leaves** round, large, toothed all the
way around, fleshy, on long, slender petioles, not numerous, all basal.

Streambanks, lakeshores, wet meadows.

AK YT

Saxifraga cespitosa

TUFTED ALPINE SAXIFRAGE

Tufted perennial herb from branched base, mat-forming. **Flowers** white to cream, several terminal on stem; petals 5, rather broad. **Stems** erect (2–6 inches), with a few tiny, toothed stem leaves. **Leaves** fan-shaped, spatulate, with 3–5 teeth at tip, hairy, densely tufted and matted in a basal rosette in which old leaves also persist.

Rocky slopes, sandy tundra, often on limestone.

AK **YT**

LAURALASKA66

LAURALASKA66

JASON GRANT

Saxifraga eschscholtzii

CUSHION SAXIFRAGE

Densely tufted perennial herb, forming compact, hemispherical cushions. **Flowers** yellow, in small clusters at top of stem; petals very tiny. **Stems** erect (about 1½ inches), slender and threadlike. **Leaves** tiny (¼ inch), pointed, margins fringed with hairs, in dense basal tufts with dry leaves of previous year.

This is a tiny, dwarf, alpine plant.
Gravel banks, rocky slopes, ledges.

AK YT

JACK BINDERNAGEL

JACK BINDERNAGEL

Saxifraga funstonii

SPOTTED SAXIFRAGE

SYNONYM *Saxifraga bronchialis*
Perennial herb forming densely matted flat cushions. **Flowers** pale yellow, 3–4 on short stems in a branched, open head; petals 5, with orange spots inside. **Stems** erect (about 6 inches), slender, with small, alternate, stem leaves. **Leaves** lanceolate to linear, pointed, very small, margins fringed with hairs, in a crowded, tufted, basal rosette.

Cliffs, rock ledges, alpine ridges, gravelly flats.

AK **YT**

285 ■

PAUL PRIOR

LAURALASKA66

THIERRY ARBAULT

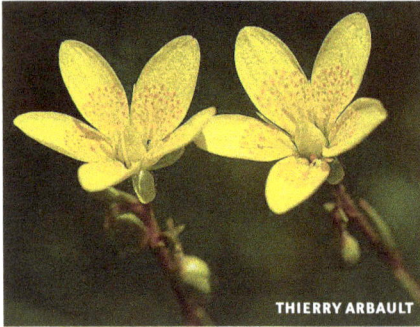

Saxifraga hirculus

YELLOW MARSH SAXIFRAGE

Perennial herb from a branched base and fibrous roots. **Flowers** yellow, sometimes red-spotted near base; 1–4 terminal on stem; petals 5, oval. **Stems** erect (about 4 inches), with several small alternate stem leaves. **Leaves** linear, blunt, smooth-edged, tapering to a long, thick petiole; mostly basal in a tuft.

Wet meadows, bogs, tundra.

AK YT

■ 286

IDA B. D'JACOBSEN

INGVILD RISKA

THIERRY ARBAULT

Saxifraga oppositifolia

PURPLE SAXIFRAGE

Tufted perennial herb forming thick cushions. **Flowers** single, at ends of leafy
branches; petals bright pink-purple to blue-
purple (or rarely white). **Flowering stems**
to 2 inches tall. **Stem leaves** small, opposite, persistent, overlapping in clusters on
non-flowering shoots; **basal leaves** absent.

Plants generally smooth but the leaves
and calyx are fringed with bristles.

Gravelly slopes and ridges, tundra.

AK YT

287 ∎

Saxifraga tricuspidata

PRICKLY SAXIFRAGE

Perennial herb, forming densely matted flat cushions. **Flowers** cream-white, occasionally dotted with orange-red; several flowers in a branched, loose, terminal head; petals 5 oval. **Stems** erect (4–8 inches), with a few alternate, tiny, toothed stem leaves. **Leaves** small, with three hard, sharp points at tip, fleshy, rigid, hairy; in a crowded basal tuft with old, matted leaves persisting.

Dry, rocky subalpine and alpine slopes, cliffs.

AK YT

ERIC LAMB

BRANDON CORDER

EERO KOSKINEN

Tofieldia coccinea

PURPLE FEATHERLING

Perennial herb from a short rhizome. **Flowers** greenish white, tinged with red or purple, cup-shaped, of 6 distinct tepals, in a head-like terminal cluster. **Stems** erect (6 inches), smooth, often purplish in the upper part. **Basal leaves** several to many, in fan-like tufts, broadly linear, smooth, sheathing at the base, folded in iris-like fashion, margins entire; **stem leaves** usually 1, bract-like, at or above middle of stem.

Rocky alpine tundra, especially on calcium-rich soils.

AK YT

289 ■

JURAJ AHEL

ANDREJUS GAIDAMAVICIUS

NICK BUTCHER

Urtica dioica

STINGING NETTLE

Perennial herb from stout rhizomes. **Flowers** greenish yellow, very small, in rather long, slender strings from a tall spike. **Stems** erect (about 2 feet), slender. **Leaves** lanceolate, with sharply serrated margins, opposite on stem, tapering at base to a petiole.

Plants covered with stinging hairs, avoid direct contact.

Thickets, streambanks, open woods.

AK YT

■ 290

BRYN

MARY LATA

PETER CASEY

Sambucus racemosa

RED ELDERBERRY

Large deciduous shrub. **Flowers** creamy white, very tiny and bell-like, ill-scented, in large, compound peaked clusters; followed in early September by bright scarlet berries. **Stems** erect (to 6 feet), branched, with stout stems. **Leaves** pinnate (5–7 leaflets), large, pointed, smooth green with slight down on underside.

Fruit ripens in August, inedible; the seeds and leaves are reported to be poisonous.

Woods, mountain slopes, streambanks, thickets.

AK **YT**

SHAAN AROESTE

ERIC LAMB

Viburnum edule

SQUASHBERRY

Deciduous shrub, spreading from rhizomes and by layering. **Flowers** white, tiny, in loose, flat clusters on short branches; followed by a red-orange berry with a large, flat seed; petals 5. **Stems** erect (to 6 feet), branched, straggling. **Leaves** 3-lobed, margins toothed, on a short petiole, resembling a maple leaf, brownish green until fully open.

Berries sour, but used in jelly and in combination with other fruits.

Moist woods, alpine slopes, streambanks, bogs.

AK **YT**

STELLA FISH

ROBERT V TAYLOR

JON

Viola adunca

HOOK-SPUR VIOLET

Perennial herb from a rhizome, stolons absent. **Flowers** pale lavender to purple, with a short spur, some flowers from leaf axils. **Stems** erect, short, branched, delicate. **Leaves** ovate to heart-shaped, small, almost no sinus, on a long petiole from the rootstock.

Moist woods, thickets, meadows.

AK YT

293 ■

HUMON

CALEB CATTO

MACHAUT₂

Viola glabella

STREAM VIOLET

Perennial herb from a rhizome, stolons absent. **Flowers** yellow, small, short spurred, solitary from leaf axils. **Stems** erect, several from rootstock, rather weak. **Leaves** broad but pointed, small, few.

Moist woods, meadows, alpine tundra; coastal areas of southern Alaska.

AK

MATT MUIR

MATT MUIR

LAURALASKA66

Viola langsdorfii

ALASKA VIOLET

Perennial herb from a rhizome, stolons absent. **Flowers** deep-purple, solitary, petals somewhat striped, spurs short,. **Stems** erect (to 6 inches), slender. **Leaves** oval to kidney-shaped, margins slightly scalloped, glabrous, on a long petiole.

Blooms fairly early (mid-June), and when found in deep grass is rather long-stemmed. Streambanks, woods, alpine meadows.

AK YT

FAMILY SYNOPSES

In lieu of a lengthy key to the families of vascular plants found in Alaska and the Yukon Territory, below are brief descriptions of the plant families included in this work. Family characteristics refer to plants present in the region. Once one is able to recognize plant families in the field, identification of unknown plants becomes much easier.

AMARANTHACEAE
Amaranth Family, 10–11

Annual herbs; leaves simple, alternate; flowers small, aggregated into spikes or heads, in some species with conspicuous colored bracts; sepals usually 5; petals absent; fruit a 1-seeded utricle. Amaranthaceae now includes former members of the Chenopodiaceae.

AMARYLLIDACEAE
Daffodil Family, 12

Perennial herb, from an onion-like bulb; leaves basal, linear; flowers in a tightly clustered pink-purple head.

APIACEAE
Carrot Family, 13–19

Biennial or perennial aromatic herbs with usually hollow stems, some very toxic; leaves alternate and sometimes also from base of plant, mostly compound; petioles sheathing stems; flowers small, perfect, in flat-topped or rounded umbrella-like clusters (umbels); petals 5, white or greenish; fruit 2-chambered.

ARACEAE
Arum Family, 20

Perennial wetland herbs; ours with a conspicuous white spathe subtending a cylindric spike of flowers (*Calla*).

ARALIACEAE
Ginseng Family, 21

Coarse, thorny shrub (*Oplopanax*); leaves lobed; flowers small, in an elongate inflorescence; fruit a red berry.

ASPARAGACEAE
Asparagus Family, 22

Perennial herb (*Maianthemum*); leaves alternate in two rows; flowers white, in a terminal cluster; fruit a round berry, blue-black when mature.

ASTERACEAE
Aster Family, 23–66

Annual, biennial or perennial herbs; leaves simple or compound, opposite, alternate, or whorled; flowers perfect or single-sexed (sometimes sterile) and of 2 types: ray (or ligulate) and disk (or tubular); ay flowers joined at base and have a long, flat, segment above (the ray); disk flowers tube-shaped with 5 lobes or teeth at tip; flowers clustered in 1 of 3 types of heads resembling a single flower and attached to a common surface (receptacle): ray flowers only (as in dandelion, *Taraxacum*); disk flowers only (discoid, as in sagebrush, *Artemisia*); and heads with both ray and disk flowers (radiate), the ray flowers surrounding the disk flowers (as in fleabane, *Erigeron*).

BALSAMINACEAE
Jewel-Weed Family, 67

Thin-leaved plants with watery juice and pendent, brightly colored irregular flowers; seedpod, when ripe, pops open when touched to eject the seeds.

BORAGINACEAE
Borage Family, 68–71

Annual or perennial herbs with often bristly stems and alternate, bristly leaves; flowers typically in a spirally coiled, spike-like head that uncurls as flowers mature.

BRASSICACEAE
Mustard Family, 72–82

Annual, biennial, or perennial herbs; leaves simple or compound, alternate on stems or basal; flowers with 4 sepals and 4 yellow, white, pink or purple petals; fruit a cylindrical (silique) or round (silicle) pod with 2 chambers.

CAMPANULACEAE
Bellflower Family, 83–85
Perennial herbs; leaves simple, alternate; flowers in racemes at ends of stems or single from upper leaf axils, perfect, 5-parted, funnel-shaped; petals blue or purple.

CAPRIFOLIACEAE
Honeysuckle Family, 86–88
Low trailing shrubs (*Linnaea*); or perennial herbs (*Valeriana*), with basal and opposite leaves; flowers in a terminal pair or cluster; perfect, 5-parted; fruit a dry capsule or achene. Family now includes members of the former Valerianaceae (*Valeriana*).

CARYOPHYLLACEAE
Pink Family, 89–94
Annual or perennial herbs; leaves simple, entire, mostly opposite but sometimes alternate or whorled; stems often swollen at nodes; flowers perfect or imperfect, in open or compact heads at ends of stems or from leaf axils; fruit a few- to many-seeded capsule.

CELASTRACEAE
Bittersweet Family, 95–96
Perennial herbs; leaves basal; flowers white, 5-parted, single at end of stem; fruit a dry capsule.

CORNACEAE
Dogwood Family, 97
Shrubs or perennial herbs (woody at base); flowers 4- or 5-parted. Fruit a drupe.

CRASSULACEAE
Stonecrop Family, 98
Plants succulent; leaves simple; flowers deep red, in a dense terminal cluster.

CYPERACEAE
Sedge Family, 99–101
Mostly perennial, grasslike, rushlike or reedlike plants; stems 3-angled, or more or less round in section, solid or pithy; leaves 3-ranked or reduced to sheaths at base of stem; leaf blades, when present, grasslike, parallel-veined, often keeled; sheaths mostly closed around the stem; flowers small, perfect or single-sexed, each flower subtended by a bract (scale); perianth of 1 to many (often 6) small bristles, or a single perianth scale, or absent; in *Carex* (not treated here), ovary within a saclike covering (perigynium), maturing into an achene, stigmas 3 or 2; flowers arranged in spikelets (termed spikes in *Carex*), the spikelets single as a terminal or lateral spike, or several to many in various types of heads, the head often subtended by one to several bracts.

DIAPENSIACEAE
Pincushion-Plant Family, 102
Dwarf subshrub; leaves evergreen, thick and shiny, in whorls along stem; flowers single at end of stem, white.

ELAEAGNACEAE
Oleaster Family, 103–104
Shrubs or trees; leaves opposite or alternate, covered with small scales (lepidote); flowers small, solitary or clustered, perfect or unisexual, petals none.

EQUISETACEAE
Horsetail Family, 105
Rushlike herbs with dark rhizomes; stems annual or perennial, grooved, usually with large central cavity and smaller outer cavities, unbranched or with whorls of branches at nodes; leaves reduced to scales, united into a sheath at each node.

ERICACEAE
Heath Family, 106–129
Ericaceae now includes former members of Pyrolaceae. Traditional Ericaceae are shrubs; leaves evergreen or deciduous, mostly alternate, simple; flowers urn- or vase-shaped, mostly white, pink, or cream-colored; fruit a berry or dry capsule. Former Pyrolaceae (*Moneses, Orthilia, Pyrola*) are perennial herbs or half-shrubs, most de-

FAMILY SYNOPSES

pendent on wood-rotting fungi (mycotrophic); leaves alternate to sometimes opposite or nearly whorled, often shiny, evergreen or deciduous; flowers 5-parted, waxy and nodding; fruit a capsule.

FABACEAE
Pea Family, 130–145
Biennial to perennial herbs; leaves alternate, pinnately divided, the terminal leaflet sometimes modified as a tendril (Vicia); flowers in simple or branched racemes, irregular; ovary maturing into a pod.

GENTIANACEAE
Gentian Family, 146–150
Annual, biennial or perennial herbs; plants usually glabrous; leaves simple, entire, opposite or whorled; flowers often showy, single at end of stems or in clusters; petals 4-5, blue, purple, white or green, joined for at least part of their length; fruit a 2-chambered, many-seeded capsule enclosed by the withered, persistent petals.

GERANIACEAE
Geranium Family, 151–152
Perennial herbs; leaves opposite, palmately lobed; flowers in a terminal cluster, petals 5, pink to purple; fruit a 4-parted capsule.

GROSSULARIACEAE
Currant Family, 153–157
Shrubs; stems smooth, or with spines at nodes and sometimes also with bristles between nodes; leaves alternate, palmately veined and palmately lobed; flowers one to several in clusters, or few to many in racemes; green to white or yellow; fruit a many-seeded berry, usually topped by persistent, dry flower parts.

IRIDACEAE
Iris Family, 158
Perennial herbs spreading by with rhizomes; leaves parallel-veined, narrow, 2-ranked, the margins joined to form an edge facing the stem (equitant); flowers with 6 petal-like segments, single or in clusters at ends of stem; fruit a 3-chambered capsule.

LAMIACEAE
Mint Family, 159–160
Perennial, often aromatic, herbs; stems 4-angled; leaves opposite; flowers solitary in leaf axils; corolla blue, 2-lipped.

LENTIBULARIACEAE
Bladderwort Family, 161
Insectivorous herbs; leaves in a basal rosette (Pinguicula); flowers 2-lipped, sometimes with a spur, 1 to several on an erect stem; fruit a capsule.

LILIACEAE
Lily Family, 162–164
Perennial herbs, from bulbs or rhizomes; leaves linear to ovate, usually from base of plant, sometimes along stem, opposite or whorled; flowers regular; sepals and petals of 6 petal-like tepals; fruit a capsule or round berry. Many former genera in the Liliaceae now placed into various new familes.

LINACEAE
Flax Family, 165
Annual or perennial herbs; leaves simple, alternate or opposite, narrow, petioles absent; flowers regular, perfect, 5- parted, petals yellow or blue; fruit a 10-chambered capsule.

MELANTHIACEAE
False Hellebore Family, 166–167
Perennial herbs (ours toxic if eaten); leaves all basal or numerous along the stem, linear to broadly oval; flowers white or greenish, in a branched or unbranched inflorescence; fruit a capsule.

MENYANTHACEAE
Buckbean Family, 168–169
Perennial wetland herbs; leaves entire or palmately divided into 3 leaflets; flowers in a raceme on a leafless stalk; petals 5, white.

MONTIACEAE
Candy-Flower Family, 170
Now includes Claytonia, formerly within Portulacaceae; plants from tubers; petals 5,

white to pink, often with pink veins.

NYMPHAEACEAE
Water-Lily Family, 171–172
Aquatic perennial herbs; stems long and fleshy, from rhizomes rooted in bottom mud; leaves large, leathery, mostly floating or emergent above water surface, heart-shaped to shield-shaped, notched at base; flowers showy, single on long stalks and borne at or above water surface, white or yellow; petals numerous; fruit a many-seeded, berrylike capsule, opening underwater when mature.

ONAGRACEAE
Evening-Primrose Family, 173–176
Perennial herbs; leaves opposite to alternate; flowers usually large and showy, in leaf axils or in heads at ends of stems; petals 4, white, yellow, or pink to rose-purple; fruit a 4-chambered capsule; seeds many, with or without a tuft of hairs (coma).

ORCHIDACEAE
Orchid Family, 177–183
Perennial herbs, from fleshy or tuberous roots, corms, or bulbs; leaves simple, along the stem and alternate, or mostly at base of plant, stalkless and usually sheathing the stem, parallel-veined; flowers irregular, showy in some species, in heads of 1 or 2 flowers at ends of stems, or with several to many flowers in a spike, raceme or panicle, each flower usually subtended by a bract; fruit a many-seeded capsule, opening by longitudinal slits (remaining closed at tip and base); seeds minute.

OROBANCHACEAE
Broom-Rape Family, 184–195
Annual to perennial herbs; often at least partially parasitic on roots of other plants; leaves opposite, alternate, or reduced to scales; flowers single or few from leaf axils, or numerous in clusters at ends of stems or leaf axils, usually with a distinct upper and lower lip; fruit a capsule; now includes many former members of Scrophulariaceae.

PAPAVERACEAE
Poppy Family, 196–199
Annual, biennial, or perennial herbs, with watery, milky, or colored juice; leaves basal or alternate on stem, dissected; flowers regular (*Papaver*), petals 4 or more, showy; fruit a capsule. The Fumariaceae, now included as a subfamily of Papaveraceae, differ in bilateral symmetry of the flowers and having stems with watery juice.

PHRYMACEAE
Lopseed Family, 200
Perennial herbs; corolla yellow, funnel-shaped and 2-lipped; calyx tubular, 5-lobed; fruit a capsule.

PLANTAGINACEAE
Plantain Family, 201–207
Perennial herbs; leaves simple, entire, all from base of plant, and flowers perfect in a narrow spike (*Plantago*). Plantaginaceae now includes not only the plantains, but also many genera formerly placed in Scrophulariaceae (such as *Veronica*).

POLEMONIACEAE
Phlox Family, 208–210
Perennial herbs; leaves opposite (*Phlox*) or pinnately divided (*Polemonium*); flowers single or in clusters at ends of stems and from leaf axils; sepals and petals 5-parted and joined for part of length; fruit a 3-chambered capsule, with usually 1 seed per chamber.

POLYGONACEAE
Buckwheat Family, 211–219
Annual or perennial herbs; leaves alternate, simple, sometimes wavy-margined, otherwise entire, the nodes usually enlarged; stipules joined to form a membranous or papery sheath (ocrea) around stem at each node; flowers in spike-like racemes or small clusters from leaf axils, or in crowded panicles at ends of stems, petals absent; in *Rumex*, sepals green to brown, in inner and outer groups, each group with 3

sepals, the 3 inner enlarging after flowering, becoming broadly winged, persisting to enclose the achene; in other genera of family, sepals more or less petal-like, white to pink or yellow.

PRIMULACEAE
Primrose Family, 220–225

Annual, biennial, or perennial herbs; leaves mostly basal (opposite or whorled in *Lysimachia*); flowers regular, mostly in clusters at ends of stems; petals mostly 5, colors varying from pink, to white or yellow; fruit a capsule.

RANUNCULACEAE
Buttercup Family, 226–245

Mostly perennial, aquatic or terrestrial herbs, leaves usually alternate, sometimes opposite or whorled, or all at base of plant; flowers mostly white or yellow, usually with 5 (occasionally more) separate petals and sepals, stamens usually numerous; pistils several to many, ripening into beaked achenes or dry capsules (follicles).

ROSACEAE
Rose Family, 246–272

Small tree (*Sorbus*), shrubs (sometimes dwarf shrubs as in *Dryas*), and annual to perennial herbs; leaves evergreen or deciduous, mostly alternate and simple or compound; flowers regular, with 5 sepals and petals; stamens numerous; fruit an achene, capsule, or fleshy fruit with numerous embedded seeds (drupe), or a fleshy fruit with seeds within (pome).

RUBIACEAE
Madder Family, 273–274

Perennial herbs; leaves simple, whorled; flowers small, perfect, white to green, single or several in loose or round clusters; fruit a capsule.

SALICACEAE
Willow Family, 275

Deciduous shrubs with alternate leaves; both staminate and pistillate flowers in catkins (aments); fruit a capsule; seeds with a dense coma of long, mostly white, silky hairs (these aid in wind-dispersal).

SANTALACEAE
Sandalwood Family, 276

Perannial herbs, parasitic on roots of other plants; leaves simple, alternate; flowers perfect or unisexual, in small axillary clusters; fruit a berry-like orange drupe.

SAXIFRAGACEAE
Saxifrage Family, 277–288

Perennial herbs, with many species found in alpine areas; leaves alternate, opposite or basal; inflorescence various, flowers regular, sepals and petals mostly 5 (4 in *Chrysosplenium*).

TOFIELDIACEAE
Featherling Family, 289

Perennial herbs with smooth or glandular-hairy stems; leaves basal and sometimes also along stem, sword-shaped; flowers 6-parted, white or greenish, in terminal clusters; fruit a rounded capsule.

URTICACEAE
Nettle Family, 290

Perennial herbs with stinging hairs; leaves opposite, simple, with petioles; flowers small, green, in branched clusters from leaf axils, staminate and pistillate flowers usually separate, on same or separate plants; fruit an achene.

VIBURNACEAE
Viburnum Family, 291–292

Family now includes shrubby genera, *Sambucus* and *Viburnum*, previously placed in Caprifoliaceae.

VIOLACEAE
Violet Family, 293–295

Perennial herbs; leaves simple, basal and sometimes alternate along stem; flowers irregular, axillary or basal, usually nodding; lower petal usually spurred or larger than the others; fruit a capsule.

GLOSSARY

Technical terms used in this book have been kept to a minimum, and those used are defined in the following glossary. Terms used to describe habitats are also defined.

acid Having more hydrogen ions than hydroxyl (OH) ions; a pH less than 7.

acute Gradually tapered to a tip.

adventive Not native to and not fully established in a new habitat.

alkaline Having more hydroxyl ions than hydrogen ions; a pH greater than 7.

alluvial Deposits of rivers and streams.

alpine high-elevation areas above treeline.

alternate Borne singly at each node, as in leaves on a stem.

ament Spikelike inflorescence of same-sexed flowers (either male or female); same as catkin.

angiosperm A plant producing flowers and bearing seeds in an ovary.

annual A plant that completes its life cycle in one growing season, then dies.

anther Pollen-bearing part of stamen, usually at the end of a stalk called a filament.

anthesis The period during which a flower is fully open and functional.

anthocyanic Pigmented with anthocyanins, this usually manifested as a tinge or suffusion of pink, red, or purple.

apomixis Clonal reproduction via seeds. Ovules are not fertilized, yet develop into viable seeds that are genetically identical to the mother plant.

appressed Lying flat to or parallel to a surface.

aquatic Living in water.

areole In leaves, the spaces between small veins.

aril A specialized appendage on a seed, often brightly colored, derived from the seed coat.

armed Bearing a sharp projection such as a prickle, spine, or thorn.

aromatic Strongly scented.

ascending Angled upward.

asymmetrical Not symmetrical.

attenuate Tapering gradually to a prolonged tip.

auricle An ear-shaped appendage to a leaf or stipule.

auriculate Having ear shaped appendages (auricles).

awl-shaped Tapering gradually from a broad base to a sharp point.

awn A thin, pointed appendage often attached at the tip.

axil Angle between a stem and the attached leaf.

barb Sharp, thorn-like projection.

basal From base of plant.

basal rosette Leaves attached to the base of the plant in a circular arrangement; plants with basal rosettes often lack stem leaves.

basic A pH greater than 7.

berry Fruit with the seeds surrounded by fleshy material.

biennial A plant that completes its life cycle in two growing season, typically flowering and fruiting in the second year, then dying.

bipinnate Leaves 2 times pinnately compound.

blade Expanded, usually flat part of a leaf or petiole.

bloom A whitish powdery or waxy coating that can be rubbed away.

bog A wet, acidic, nutrient-poor peatland characterized by sphagnum and other mosses, shrubs and sedges. Technically, a type of peatland raised above its surroundings by peat accumulation and receiving nutrients only from precipitation.

boreal Far northern latitudes.

brackish Salty.

bract A modified leaf (often leaf-like, sometimes scale-like) at the base of a flower or inflorescence; often reduced.

bristle A stiff hair.

bud An undeveloped shoot, inflorescence, or flower, in woody plants often covered by scales and serving as the overwintering stage.

bulb A group of modified leaves serving as a foodstorage organ, borne on a short, vertical, underground stem (compare with corm).

bulbil A bulb-like structure borne in the leaf axils or in place of flowers.

bulblet Small bulb borne above ground, as in a leaf axil.

caespitose Plants that grow in dense tufts or cushions (also spelled *cespitose*).

calcareous fen An uncommon wetland type associated with seepage areas, and which receive groundwater enriched with primarily calcium and magnesium bicarbonates.

calciphile Plants that like to grow in lime-rich soils.

calcium-rich Refers to soils underlain by limestone or receiving water enriched by calcium compounds.

calyx The flower whorl that consists of all the sepals, often used when the sepals are fused together.

campanulate Bell-shaped.

capitate Abruptly expanded at the apex, thereby forming a knob-like tip.

capsule A dry dehiscent fruit that was derived from more than 1 carpel.

carpel Part of the female reproductive organ, consisting of an ovary, style and stigma; multiple carpels can be fused.

caryopsis The dry, indehiscent seed of grasses.

catkin Spikelike inflorescence of same-sexed flowers (either male or female); same as ament.

caudex Firm, hardened, summit of a root mass that functions as a perennating organ.

cauline Of or pertaining to the above-ground portion of the stem.

cespitose Growing in a compact cluster with closely spaced stems; tufted, clumped (also spelled *caespitose*).

chaff Thin, dry scales; in the Asteraceae, sometimes found as chaffy bracts on the receptacle.

cilia Hairs found at the margin of an organ.

ciliate With hairs along the margin.

circumboreal Refers to a species distribution pattern which circles the earth's boreal regions.

circumpolar Occurring in the arctic around the Northern Hemisphere.

clasping Leaves that partially encircle the stem at the base.

clavate Widened in the distal portion, like a baseball bat.

claw The narrow, basal portion of perianth parts.

cleistogamous Type of flower that remains closed and is self-pollinated.

clumped Having the stems grouped closely together; tufted.

colony-forming A group of plants of the same species, produced either vegetatively or by seed.

column The joined style and filaments in the Orchidaceae.

coma A tuft of fine hairs, especially at the tip of a seed.

composite An inflorescence that is made up of many tiny florets crowded together on a receptacle; members of the Aster Family (Asteraceae).

compound leaf A leaf with two or more leaflets.

concave Curved inward.

cone The dry fruit of conifers composed of overlapping scales.

conifer Cone-bearing woody plants.

convex Curved outward.

convolute Arranged such that one edge is covered and the other is exposed, usually referring to petals in bud.

cordate With a rounded lobe on each side of a central sinus; heart-shaped.

coriaceous With a firm, leathery texture.

corm A short, vertical, enlarged, underground stem that serves as a food storage organ (compare with bulb).

corolla The flower whorl that consists of all the petals, often used when the petals are fused together.

corymb A flat topped cluster of flowers; the lower branches or pedicels have longer stems, leading to the flowers being produced at the same height.

crenate Rounded toothed margins; generally used to describe leaf margins.

crenulate Finely crenate.

crisped An irregularly crinkled or curled leaf margin.

crown Persistent base of a plant, especially a grasses.

culm The stem of a grass or grasslike plant, especially a stem with the inflorescence.

cyme A type of inflorescence in which the central flowers open first.

deciduous Plants that lose their leaves in fall; not evergreen.

decumbent A stem that is prostrate at the base and curves upward to have an erect or ascending, apical portion.

decurrent Possessing an adnate line or wing that extends down the axis below the node, usually referring to leaves on a stem.

dehiscent Opening up at maturity; generally referring to fruit or anthers.

deltate Triangle-shaped.

deltoid Triangular.

dentate Provided with outward oriented teeth.

depauperate Poorly developed due to unfavorable conditions.

dicots One of two main divisions of the Angiosperms (the other being the Monocots); plants having 2 seed leaves (cotyledons), net-venation, and flower parts in 4's or 5's (or multiples of these numbers).

dioecious Bearing only male or female flowers on a single plant.

disjunct A population of plants widely separated from its main range.

disk In the Asteraceae, the central part of the head, composed of tubular flowers (also spelled *disc*).

dissected Leaves divided into many smaller segments.

disk floret Flowers of the Asteraceae family; with a less prominent fused corolla with 5 lobes; in flowers with both ray florets and disk florets, these are in the center of the flowering head.

discoid In composite flowers (Asteraceae), a head with only disk (tubular) flowers, the ray flowers absent.

disturbed Natural communities altered by human influences.

divided Leaves which are lobed nearly to the midrib.

dolomite A type of limestone consisting of calcium magnesium carbonate.

dorsal Underside, or back of an organ.

drupe A fleshy fruit with a single large seed such as a cherry.

eglandular Without glands.

elliptic Broadest at the middle, gradually tapering to both ends.

emergent Growing out of and above the water surface.

endemic A species restricted to a particular region.

entire Margins containing no serrations, smooth.

erect Stiffly upright.

escape A cultivated plant which establishes itself outside of cultivation.

evergreen Plant retaining its leaves throughout the year.

excurrent With the central rib or axis continuing or projecting beyond the organ.

exserted Extending beyond the mouth of a structure, such as stamens extending out from mouth of corolla.

falcate Sickle-shaped.

fellfield A slope that due to the snow and wind give these plants characteristic forms; usually references alpine slopes and their respective plants.

fen An open wetland usually dominated by herbaceous plants, and fed by in-flowing, often calcium- and/or magnesium-rich water; soils vary from peat to clays and silts.

fern Perennial plants with spore-bearing leaves similar to the vegetative leaves and bearing sporangia on their underside, or the spore-bearing leaves much modified.

fibrous A cluster of slender roots, all with the same diameter.

filament The stalk of a stamen which supports the anther.

filiform Thread-like.

floating mat A feature of some ponds where plant roots form a carpet over some or all of the water surface.

floodplain That part of a river valley that is occasionally covered by flood waters.

floret A small flower in a dense cluster of flowers; in grasses the flower with its attached lemma and palea.

floricane the second-year flowering stem of *Rubus* (compare with primocane).

follicle A dry fruit that was derived from a single carpel and splits open from a single side.

genus The first part of the scientific name for a plant or animal (plural *genera*).

glabrate Nearly glabrous or becoming so.

glabrous Without hair.

gland An appendage or depression which produces a sticky or greasy substance.

glandular Outgrowths that secrete, such as hairs that produce compounds to deter grazing or sticky substances that trap insects.

glaucous With a waxy residue, usually whitish or bluish in color.

grain The fruit of a grass; the swollen seed-like protuberance on the fruit of some *Rumex*.

gymnosperm Plants in which the seeds are not produced in an ovary, but usually in a cone.

halophyte A plant adapted to growing in a salty substrate.

hardwoods Loosely used to contrast most deciduous trees from conifers.

hastate Shaped like an arrowhead with the bottom lobes facing outwards; compare saggitate.

haustorium A specialized, root-like connection to a host plant that a parasite uses to extract nourishment.

heath open areas with highly organic soils.

herb A herbaceous, non-woody plant.

herbaceous Like an herb; also, leaflike in appearance.

hirsute Pubescent with coarse, somewhat stiff, usually curving hairs, coarser than villous but softer than hispid.

hispid Pubescent with coarse, stiff hairs that may be uncomfortable to the touch, coarser than hirsute but softer than bristly.

hummock A small, raised mound formed by certain species of sphagnum moss.

humus Dark, well-decayed organic matter in soil.

hybrid A cross-breed between two species.

hydric Wet (compare with mesic, xeric).

hygroscopic Attracting and absorbing water molecules.

hypanthium A ring, cup, or tube around the ovary; the sepals, petals and stamens are attached to the rim of the hypanthium.

imbricate Overlapping, as shingles on a roof. In flowers with ray and disk florets, these make up the outer margin of the flowering head.

indehiscent Not splitting open at maturity.

inferior The position of the ovary when it is below the point of attachment of the sepals and petals.

inflorescence A part of the plant where the flowers are arranged.

insectivorous Refers to the insect trapping and digestion habit of some plants as a nutrition supplement.

internode The space on a stem between each node; see node.

introduced A non-native species.

invasive Non-native species causing significant ecological or economic problems.

involucral bract A single member of the involucre; sometimes called phyllary in composite flowers (Asteraceae).

involucre A whorl of bracts, subtending a flower or inflorescence.

involucrum A whorl of bracts that subtend a flower or inflorescence.

involute Leaf margins rolling inwards towards the upper side of the leaf.

irregular flower Not radially symmetric; with similar parts unequal.

joint A node or section of a stem where the branch and leaf meet.

keel A central rib like the keel of a boat. The length-wise fusion between the lower petals of a flower from the Pea Family (Fabaceae).

laciniate Irregularly dissected into narrow lobes.

lance-shaped Broadest near the base, gradually tapering to a narrower tip.

lanceolate Sword shaped; wider at the base than the tip.

lateral Borne on the sides of a stem or branch.

lax Loose or drooping.

leaf axil The point of the angle between a stem and a leaf.

leaflet One of the leaflike segments of a compound leaf.

lens-shaped Biconvex in shape (like a lentil).

lenticel Blisterlike openings in the epidermis of woody stems, admitting gases to and from the plant, and often appearing as small oval dots on bark.

ligulate Having a ligule; in the Asteraceae, the strap-shaped corolla of a ray floret.

ligule Either the membranous or hairy appendage at the base of a grass leaf; or, the strap-shaped petals of some flowers in the Asteraceae family.

linear Thin and elongate with parallel sides.

lip Upper or lower part of a 2-lipped corolla; also the lower petal in most orchid flowers.

lobed With lobes; in leaves, divisions usually not over halfway to the midrib.

local Occurring sporadically in an area.

lyrate A leaf that is lobed where the terminal lobe is much larger than the lower lobes.

margin The outer edge of a leaf.

marl A calcium-rich clay.

marsh Wetland dominated by herbaceous plants, with standing water for part or all the growing season, then often drying at the surface.

meadow Moist open areas dominated by herbaceous plants; trees and shrubs typically sparse or absent.

mesic Moist, neither dry nor wet (compare with hydric, xeric).

midrib The prominent vein along the main axis of a leaf.

mixed forest A type of forest composed of both deciduous and conifer trees.

moat The open water area ringing the outer edge of a peatland or floating mat.

monocots One of two main divisions of the Angiosperms (the other being the Dicots); plants with a single seed leaf (cotyledon); typically having narrow leaves with parallel veins, and flower parts in 3s or multiples of 3.

monoecious (or monecious) A plant with both male and female flowers on the same plant (imperfect or unisexual flowers) or with flowers have both male and female reproductive parts (perfect or bisexual flowers).

montane mid-elevation area below the subalpine; trees are well-developed.

muck An organic soil where the plant remains are decomposed to the point where the type of plants forming the soil cannot be determined.

mucro A sharp point at termination of an organ or other structure.

muskeg Bog dominated by sphagnum mosses with widely spaced spruce trees; a common habitat type in interior Alaska.

mycorrhizae The symbiotic relationship between fungal hyphae and plant roots.

naked Without a covering; a stalk or stem without leaves.

native An indigenous species.

naturalized An introduced species that is established and persistent in an ecosystem.

nectary Where nectar is made; usually a gland at the base of a petal or sepal.

needle A slender leaf, as in the Pinaceae.

nerve A leaf vein.

neutral A pH of 7.

node Where the stem, leaf, and flower (if any) grow on a stem; the joints of a stem.

nutlet The fruit type of mints (Lamiaceae) and borages (Boraginaceae).

obcordate Heart shaped where the attachment is at the narrower end.

oblanceolate Wider at the tip than at the base with attachment at the narrower end; inverse of lanceolate.

oblique Emerging or joining at an angle other than parallel or perpendicular.

oblong Much longer than wide with parallel sides.

obovate Egg shaped with attachment at narrower end.

ocrea A tube-shaped stipule or pair of stipules around the stem; characteristic of the Buckwheat Family (Polygonaceae).

opposite Leaves or branches which are paired opposite one another on the stem.

orbicular More or less circular in outline.

organic Soils composed of decaying plant remains.

oval Elliptical.

ovary The lower part of the pistil that produces the seeds.

ovate Broadly rounded at the base, becoming narrowed above; broader than lanceolate.

palmate Divided into more than three segments with a central point of attachment, like a hand; usually referring to leaves.

panicle An arrangement of flowers consisting of several racemes.

papilla (plural papillae) A short, rounded or cylindrical projection.

pappus The modified sepals of a composite flower which persist atop the ovary as bristles, scales or awns.

parallel-veined With several veins running from base of leaf to leaf tip, characteristic of most monocots.

peat An organic soil formed of partially decomposed plant remains.

peatland A wetland whose soil is composed primarily of organic matter (mosses, sedges, etc.); a general term for bogs and fens.

pedicel A stem of a flower in an inflorescence.

peduncle The stem of a solitary flower or an inflorescence.

peltate More or less circular, with the stalk attached at a point on the underside.

pepo A fleshy, many-seeded fruit with a tough rind, as a melon.

perennial Living for 3 or more years.

perfect A flower having both male (stamens) and female (pistils) parts.

perianth Collectively, all the sepals and petals of a flower.

permafrost a thick subsurface layer of soil that remains frozen throughout the year.

petal An individual part of the corolla, often white or colored.

petiole The stalk of a leaf.

phyllary An involucral bract subtending the flower head in composite flowers (Asteraceae).

pinnate A leaf regularly divided into segments with leaflets on either side of the axis, resembling a feather.

pinnatifid Pinnately lobed.

pistil The female reproductive organ of a flower, consisting of one or more fused carpels each with a stigma, style, and ovary. Develops into a fruit and contains ovules, which can become seeds if fertilized.

pistillate Flowers imperfect, containing only female reproductive parts. Female flowers.

pith A spongy central part of stems and branches.

pollen The male spores in an anther.

primocane The first-year, vegetative stem in *Rubus* (compare with floricane).

prostrate Lying flat on the ground.

pubescence Small hairs that are irregularly arranged and sparse.

raceme A grouping of flowers along an elongated axis where each flower has its own stalk.

rachis The central axis or stem of a leaf or inflorescence.

radiate heads In composite flowers, heads with both ray and disk flowers (Asteraceae).

ray floret Flowers of the Asteraceae with prominent strap-shaped petals.

ray flower A ligulate or strap-shaped flower in the Asteraceae, where often the outermost series of flowers in the head.

receptacle In the Asteraceae, the enlarged summit of the flower stalk to which the sepals, petals, stamens, and pistils are usually attached.

recurved Curved backward.

regular Flowers with all the similar parts of the same form.

reniform Kidney-shaped.

retuse A shallow notch at the apex.

revolute Leaf margins rolled in towards the underside.

rhizomatous Spreading by rhizomes (underground stems).

rhizome An underground, horizontal stem.

rib A pronounced vein or nerve.

root nodules Areas on roots of certain plants that house cyanobacteria to fix nitrogen.

rootstock Similar to rhizome but referring to any underground part that spreads the plant.

rosette A crowded, circular clump of leaves.

saggitate Shaped like an arrowhead with the bottom lobes facing downwards; compare hastate.

samara A dry, indehiscent fruit with a well-developed wing.

saprophyte A plant that lives off of dead organic matter.

scape A naked stem (without leaves) bearing the flowers.

secund Flowers mostly on one side of a stalk or branch.

sedge meadow A community dominated by sedges (Cyperaceae) and occurring on wet, saturated soils.

GLOSSARY

seep A spot where water oozes from the ground.

sepal The outer most whorl of a flower, often leaf-like and initially protecting the flower bud.

serotinous A condition of seed dispersal in some plants needing heat (generally produced by wildfire) to allow opening of fruit or cones to disperse seeds.

serrate Tooth like projections along the margin; usually in reference to leaves.

sessile Without a stalk, directly attached.

sheath Tube-shaped membrane around a stem, especially for part of the leaf in grasses and sedges.

shrub A woody plant with multiple stems.

silicle Short fruit of the Mustard Family (Brassicaceae), normally less than 2x longer as wide.

silique Dry, dehiscent, 2-chambered fruit, with a persistent middle septum, of the Mustard Family (Brassicaceae), longer than a silicle.

simple Not compound; a leaf that has not been divided into many leaflets.

sinus The depression between two lobes.

smooth Without teeth or hairs.

spadix A fleshy axis in which flowers are embedded.

spathe A large bract subtending or enclosing a cluster of flowers.

spatula-shaped Broadest at tip and tapering to the base.

spatulate Spatula-shaped; round at the tip and tapering towards the base.

sphagnum moss A type of moss common in peatlands and sometimes forming a continuous carpet across the surface; sometimes forming layers several meters thick; also loosely called peat moss.

spike A group of unstalked flowers along an unbranched stalk.

spikelet A small spike; the flower cluster (inflorescence) of grasses (Poaceae) and sedges (Cyperaceae). In grasses, the two outermost bracts are called glumes, and each flower inside has two more bracts, the lemma (lower) and palea (upper).

spore a one-celled reproductive structure that gives rise to the gamete-bearing plant.

spreading Widely angled outward.

spring A place where water flows naturally from the ground.

spur A hollow, pointed projection of a flower.

stamen The male reproductive organ, consisting of a filament (stalk-like appendage) and anther, which releases pollen.

staminate Imperfect flowers that contain only stamens; male flowers.

staminode An infertile stamen.

stellate Hairs that arise from a single base; looks star-shaped.

stem The main axis of a plant.

stigma The terminal, often sticky, part of a pistil which receives pollen.

stipule A leaflike outgrowth at the base of a leaf stalk.

stolon A horizontal stem lying on the soil surface that roots and buds into another individual; runners, as in strawberry plants.

stoloniferous Spreading by stolons (above-ground stems).

style The stalklike part of the pistil between the ovary and the stigma.

subalpine area located below the alpine and above the montane zones; trees often stunted and scattered.

subspecies A subdivision of the species forming a group with shared traits which differ from other members of the species (subsp., ssp.).

subtend Attached below and extending upward.

succulent Thick, fleshy and juicy.

superior Referring to the position of the ovary when it is above the point of attachment of sepals, petals, stamens, and pistils.

swale A slight depression.

swamp Wooded wetland dominated by trees or shrubs; soils are typically wet for much of year or sometimes inundated.

taiga boreal forests dominated by trees of black and white spruce and larch; in American usage, often refers to the stunted forests approaching northern limit of tree growth.

talus Fallen rock at the base of a slope or cliff.

taproot A main, downward-pointing root.

tendril A threadlike appendage from a stem or leaf that coils around other objects for support (as in *Vicia*).

tepal Sepals or petals not differentiated from one another.

terete Round in cross section.

terminal Located at the end of a stem or stalk.

ternate In orders of three.

thicket A dense growth of woody plants.

tomentose Short hairs that are densely packed together.

tomentum A felted covering of rhizoids that appears wooly.

toothed Leaf margin with saw-like indentations.

translucent Nearly transparent.

tree A large, single-stemmed woody plant.

trifoliate Leaf divided into three leaflets.

truncate Abruptly cut-off.

tuber An enlarged portion of a root or rhizome.

tundra Treeless plain in arctic regions, having permanently frozen subsoil.

turion A specialized type of shoot or bud that overwinters and resumes growth the following year.

tussock Dense hummock formed by certain grass or sedge species.

umbel A cluster of flowers in which the flower stalks arise from the same level.

umbelet A small, secondary umbel in an umbel, as in the Apiaceae.

upright Erect or nearly so.

urceolate Constricted at a point just before an opening; urn-shaped.

utricle A small, one-seeded fruit with a dry, papery outer covering.

valve A segment of a dehiscent fruit; the wing of the fruit in *Rumex*.

variety Taxon below subspecies and differing from other varieties within the same subspecies (var.).

vein A vascular bundle, as in a leaf.

venation The pattern of veins on an organ.

ventral Front side.

verrucose Covered with small, wart-like projections.

verticil One whorled cycle of organs.

verticillate Arranged in whorls.

villous Pubescent with long, soft, bent hairs, the hairs not crimped or tangled.

vine A trailing or climbing plant, dependent on other objects for support.

viscid Sticky, glutinous.

viviparous Producing bulbs that begin to develop before becoming detached from the 'mother' plant, often in the place of flowers.

whorl A group of 3 or more parts from one point on a stem.

wing A thin tissue bordering or surrounding an organ.

woody Xylem tissue (the vascular tissue which conducts water and nutrients).

xeric Dry (compare with hydric, mesic).

Linear

Lanceolate

Oblanceolate

Oblong

Elliptical

Oval

Ovate

Obovate

Spatulate

Cuneate
(Wedge-shaped)

Deltoid
(Triangular)

Cordate
(Heart-shaped)

Reniform
(Kidney-shaped)

Orbicular
(circular)

Peltate
(Shield-shaped)

Pinnately
Lobed

Pinnately
Divided

Palmately
Lobed

Palmately
Divided

Palmately much
Divided

Odd pinnate

Even pinnate

Interruptedly
pinnate

Compound
pinnate

Trifoliolate

Digitate

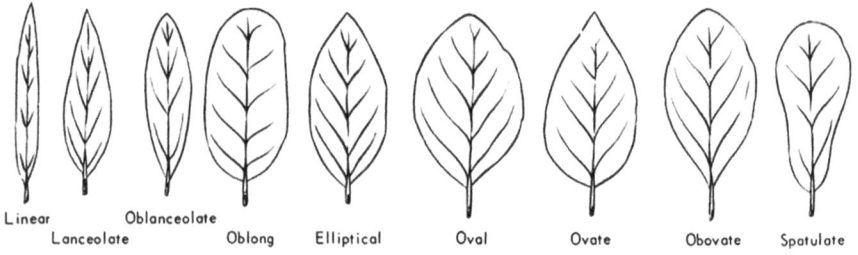

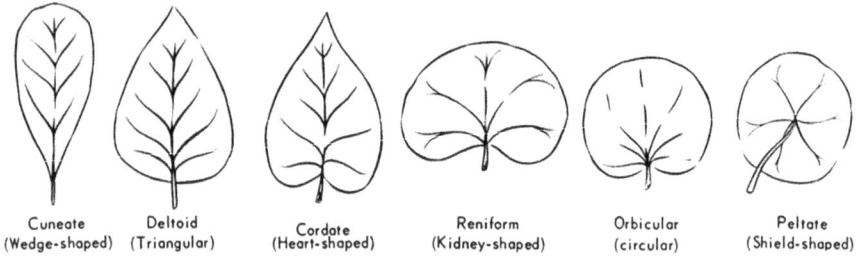

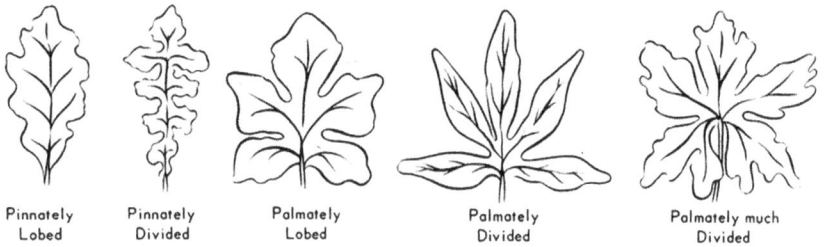

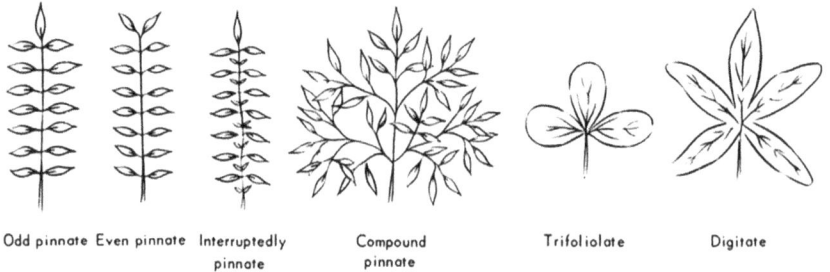

TYPICAL LEAF SHAPES.

Flowers not stalked

SPIKE

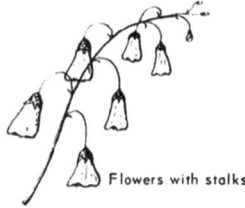

Flowers with stalks

RACEME

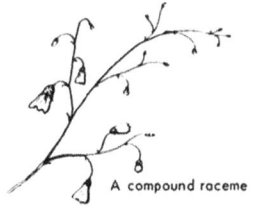

A compound raceme

PANICLE

Flower stalks from a common center

UMBEL

Terminal flowers open last

CORYMB

Terminal flowers open first

CYME

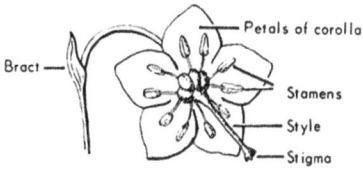

Bract

Petals of corolla

Stamens

Style

Stigma

Parts of flower of One-flowered wintergreen

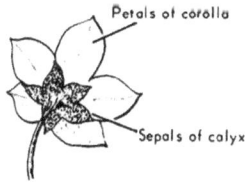

Petals of corolla

Sepals of calyx

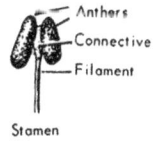

Anthers

Connective

Filament

Stamen

Superior ovary

Inferior ovary

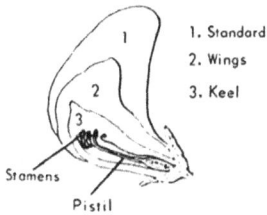

1. Standard
2. Wings
3. Keel

Stamens

Pistil

Section of flower of a legume

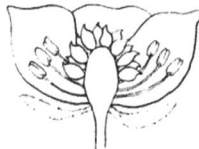

Section of flower of Buttercup

INFLORESCENCE TYPES, PARTS OF A FLOWER.

THREE-PETALED
(Arrowhead)

FOUR-PETALED
(Mustard)

FIVE-PETALED
(Chickweed)

MANY-PETALED
(Purple cactus)

URN-SHAPED
(Bearberry)

CYLINDRICAL
(Gentian)

CAMPANULATE
(Harebell)

FUNNELFORM
(Morning-glory)

SALVER-FORM
(Collomia)

ROTATE
(Wild tomato)

(Bittersweet)

REFLEXED PETALS
(Shooting star)

PAPILIONACEOUS
(Vetchling)

BILABIATE
(Marsh hedge-nettle)

(Monkeyflower)

SPURRED
(Toadflax)

(Violet)

IRREGULAR
(Low larkspur)

(Leafy spurge)

(Lady's-slipper)

TYPES OF FLOWERS.

ACORN
(oak)

NUTS
(American hazel)

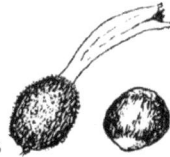
(Beaked hazel)

SAMARAS
(Elm)   (Maple)   (Ash)

DRUPES
(American plum)   (Choke cherry)

SILICLES
(Bladderpod) (Shepherd's-purse) (Stinkweed)   (Hare's-ear mustard)   (Wild radish)

SILIQUES

LEGUMES

'Milk-vetch)   (Ground-plum)   (Golden-bean)

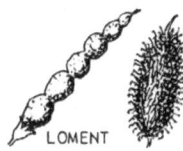  

LOMENT

(Sweet-broom) (Wild licorice)   (Vetch)

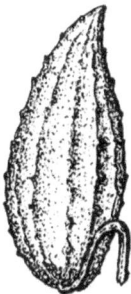

CAPSULES

Violet   (Geranium)   (Fireweed)   (Shootingstar)   (Black henbane)   (Flax)

(Milkweed)

FOLLICLES

(Low larkspur)

ACCESSORY FRUIT
(Strawberry)

AGGREGATE FRUIT
(Raspberry)

PYXIS
(Purslane)

SCHIZOCARPS
(cow parsnip) (Sweet cicely)

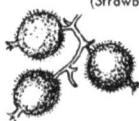
BERRIES
(Gooseberry)

BUR
(Cocklebur)

ACHENES
(Various)

TYPES OF FRUIT.

ADDITIONAL REFERENCES

Below are additional print and online references to the plants and vegetation of Alaska and the Yukon Territory.

PRINT

Anderson, J.P. 1959. *Flora of Alaska and Adjacent Parts of Canada. An illustrated descriptive text of all vascular plants known to occur within the region covered.* Iowa State University Press. Ames, Iowa.

Argus, G.W. 1973. *The Genus Salix in Alaska and the Yukon.* Publications in Botany No. 2. National Museum of Canada. Ottawa, Ontario.

Argus, G.W. 2004. *A Guide to the identification of Salix (Willows) in Alaska, the Yukon Territory, and adjacent regions.* July 2004 workshop on willow identification. Unpublished.

Chadde, S.W. 2020. *Alaska Trees and Shrubs.* Orchard Innovations Books. Mountain View, Arkansas.

Chadde, S.W. 2022. *Denali Flora.* Orchard Innovations Books. Mountain View, Arkansas.

Cody, W.J. 2000. *Flora of the Yukon Territory.* Second Edition. National Research Council of Canada Press. Ottawa, Ontario.

Collet, D. 2004. Willows of Interior Alaska. U.S. Fish and Wildlife Service.

Douglas, G.W., G.B. Straley, D.V. Meidinger, and J. Pojar. 1998. *Illustrated Flora of British Columbia.* Volumes 1–8. B.C. Ministry of Environment, Land, & Parks and B.C. Ministry of Forests. Victoria, British Columbia.

Flora of North America Editorial Committee (eds.). 1993+. *Flora of North America North of Mexico.* 20+ vols. New York & Oxford.

Garibaldi, A. 1999. *Medicinal flora of the Alaska Natives: a compilation of knowledge from literary sources of Aleut, Alutiiq,* Athabascan, Eyak, Haida, Inupiat, Tlingit, Tsimshian, and Yupik traditional healing methods using plants. Alaska Natural Heritage Program. Univ. of Alaska Anchorage.

Hitchcock, C.L., A. Cronquist, D.E. Giblin, B.S. Legler, P.F. Zika, and R.G. Olmstead. 2018. *Flora of the Pacific Northwest: An Illustrated Manual.* Second Edition. University of Washington Press. Seattle, Washington.

Hultén, E.O. 1968. *Flora of Alaska and Neighboring Territories: A Manual of the Vascular Plants.* Stanford University Press. Stanford, California.

Jernigan, K., O. Alexie, S. Alexie, M. Stover, R. Meier, C. Parker, M. Pete, and M. Rasmussen (eds.). 2015. *A Guide to the Ethnobotany of the Yukon-Kuskokwim Region.* University Of Alaska Fairbanks, Alaska Native Language Center.

Kari, P.R. 1995. *Tanaina Plantlore, Dena'ina K'et'una.* Alaska Native Language Center with Alaska Natural History Association and National Park Service.

Moerman, D.E. 1998. *Native American Ethnobotany.* Timber Press. Portland, OR.

Moerman, D.E. 2010. *Native American Food Plants: An Ethnobotanical Dictionary.* Timber Press. Portland, Oregon.

Pratt, V.E. 1989. *Field Guide to Alaskan Wildflowers.* Alaskakrafts, Inc. Anchorage, AK

Roland, C., Stehn, S., Hampton-Miller, C., and Groth, E. 2016. *Ecological Atlas of Denali's Flora.* National Park Service. Available at: ecologicalatlas.uaf.edu.

Sheviak, C.J. 1999. *The identities of Platanthera hyperborea and P. huronensis, with the description of a new species from North America.* Lindleyana 14: 193–203.

Skinner Q.D., S.J. Wright, R.J. Henszey, J.L. Henszey, and S.K. Wyman. 2012. *A Field Guide to Alaska Grasses*. Education Resources Publishing: Cumming, Georgia.

Tande G.F. and R. Lipkin. 2003. *Wetland Sedges of Alaska*. Alaska Natural Heritage Program, Environment and Natural Resources Institute, University of Alaska Anchorage.

Tolmatchev, A.I., J.G. Packer, and G.C.D. Griffiths. 1996. *Flora of the Russian Arctic*. Volumes 1–3. University of Alberta Press. Edmonton, Alberta.

Viereck, L.A., and E.L. Little. 2007. *Alaska Trees and Shrubs*. Second Edition. University of Alaska Press. Fairbanks, Alaska.

Welsh, S.L. 1974. *Anderson's Flora of Alaska and Adjacent Parts of Canada*. Brigham Young University Press. Provo, Utah.

ONLINE

Alaska Center for Conservation Science (ACCS) (accs.uaa.alaska.edu).

Alaska Native Plant Society (AKNPS) (aknps.org).

Arctic Flora of Canada and Alaska (arcticplants.myspecies.info).

Consortium of Pacific Northwest Herbaria (www.pnwherbaria.org).

E-Flora British Columbia (ibis.geog.ubc.ca/biodiversity/eflora).

Ecological Atlas of Denali's Flora, Denali National Park and Preserve (ecologicalatlas.uaf.edu).

Flora of Alaska. (floraofalaska.org).

INDEX TO PLANT FAMILIES

Scientific names of the plant families included in this book are listed below.

INDEX

Scientific (or botanical) names are listed in *italics*. Common names are listed in roman type. Family names (scientific and common) are in **bold type**.

INDEX

INDEX

INDEX

INDEX

INDEX

INDEX

www.ingramcontent.com/pod-product-compliance
Lightning Source LLC
Chambersburg PA
CBHW052108030426
42335CB00025B/2893